S H O C K S

15 Startling Stories to Shock and Delight

With Exercises for Comprehension & Enrichment

by Burton Goodman

Jamestown Publishers
Providence, Rhode Island

Shocks

Catalog No. 665

© 1994 by Burton Goodman

Cover and text design by Patricia Volpe, adapted from
the original design by Deborah Hulsey Christie
Cover illustration by Bob Eggleton

Text illustrations by
Ann G. Barrow: pp. 39, 42; Heidi Chang: pp. 54, 59, 108, 111, 114;
David Delay: p. 65; Maurice P. Dogué: pp. 46–47, 49, 78–79, 81;
Kathleen S. Dwyer: pp. 22, 25, 129, 131, 134; Lyn Fletcher: pp. 30–31,
33, 86, 90, 119, 122; Timothy C. Jones: pp. 8–9, 13, 16, 140, 143;
Pamela R. Levy: pp. 70–71, 73; James Watling: pp. 96, 101, 102

Printed in the United States of America

3 4 5 6 BP 98 97 96

ISBN 0-89061-750-3

Contents

To the Student

$\mathcal{T}$his book contains 15 exciting stories by some of the world's greatest writers. As the title suggests, each story provides a *shock*. These tales offer you hours of reading pleasure. And the exercises that follow will help you improve your reading and literature skills.

You will notice that the exercises are also based on a *shock:*

SELECTING DETAILS FROM THE STORY

HANDLING STORY ELEMENTS

OBSERVING NEW VOCABULARY WORDS

COMPLETING A CLOZE PASSAGE

KNOWING HOW TO READ CRITICALLY

SELECTING DETAILS FROM THE STORY helps you improve your reading skills.

HANDLING STORY ELEMENTS helps you understand key elements of literature. On page 7 you will find the meanings of ten important terms. If you wish, look back at those meanings when you answer the questions in this section.

OBSERVING NEW VOCABULARY WORDS helps you strengthen your vocabulary skills. Often, you can figure out the meaning of an unfamiliar word by using *context clues* in the story. Those clues are the words and phrases around the unfamiliar word. The vocabulary words in the story are printed in **boldface**. If you wish, look back at these words before you answer the questions in this section.

COMPLETING A CLOZE PASSAGE helps you strengthen your reading *and* your vocabulary skills through the use of fill-in, or cloze, exercises.

KNOWING HOW TO READ CRITICALLY helps you sharpen your critical thinking skills. You will *reason* by using story clues, making inferences (figuring things out), and drawing conclusions.

Another section, **Questions for Writing and Discussion**, gives you opportunities to think, discuss, and write about the stories.

Here is the way to do the exercises:
- There are four questions for each of the SHOCK exercises above.
- Do all the exercises.
- Check your answers with your teacher.
- Use the scoring chart at the end of each exercise to figure out your score for that exercise. Give yourself 5 points for each correct answer. (Since there are four questions, you can get up to 20 points for each exercise.)
- Use the SHOCK scoring chart at the end of the exercises to figure your total score. A perfect score for the five exercises would equal 100 points.
- Keep track of how well you do by writing in your Score Total on the Progress Chart on page 150. Then write your score on the Progress Graph on page 151 to plot your progress.

I know that you will enjoy reading the stories in this book. And the exercises that follow them will help you master some very important skills.

Now . . . get ready for some *Shocks!*

Burton Goodman

The Short Story—
10 Important Literary Terms

Characterization: how a writer shows what a character is like. The way a character acts, speaks, thinks, and looks *characterizes* that person.

Conflict: a struggle, fight, or difference of opinion between characters.

Dialogue: the words that a character says; the speech between characters.

Main Character: the person the story is mostly about.

Mood: the feeling that the writer creates. For example, the *mood* of a story might be humorous or suspenseful.

Plot: the outline, or order, of events in a story.

Purpose: the reason the author wrote the story. For example, the author's *purpose* might be to amuse the reader.

Setting: where and when the story takes place; the time and place of the action in a story.

Style: the special way that a writer uses language. How a writer arranges words, sentences, and ideas helps to create that writer's *style*.

Theme: the main idea of the story. Note that the *theme* is the central idea of the story. The *plot* is the arrangement, or order, of events.

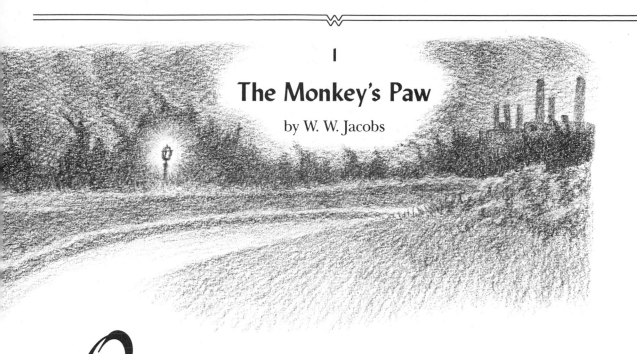

I
The Monkey's Paw

by W. W. Jacobs

Outside the night was cold and wet. But in the small house, the blinds were drawn and the fire burned brightly in the fireplace. Mr. White and his son were playing chess.

"Listen to the wind," said Mr. White, looking up suddenly.

"I'm listening," said his son, Herbert, as he stared at the board. He stretched out his arm and moved a piece. "Check," he said.

"The weather's so bad," said Mr. White. "I doubt that Sergeant Morris will come tonight."

The boy nodded and made the final move. "Checkmate!" he said.

"That's the worst part of living out here," scowled Mr. White. "Of all the out-of-the-way places to live in, this is the worst! The yard's like a lake and the path's all muddy."

"Now, now, never mind, dear," said his wife, who was knitting near the fire. "Perhaps you'll win the next game."

Just then they heard the gate banging loudly, and the sound of heavy footsteps coming toward the door.

"There he is," said Herbert.

Mr. White rose and opened the door. A tall, powerful man with bright, beady eyes, entered the room. His face was red from the cold.

"Let me introduce Sergeant Morris," said Mr. White.

The sergeant shook hands and took the seat that was offered to him near the fireplace. Mr. White put a kettle on the fire, while the sergeant warmed his hands.

After several minutes the sergeant began to talk. The little family circle listened with eager interest as he spoke of the distant places he had visited. His eyes grew even brighter as he spoke of daring deeds and strange events.

"I'd like to see India, myself," said Mr. White. "Just to look around a bit. I'd like to see those old temples. What was that you started telling me about the other day—a monkey's paw, or something, Morris?"

"Nothing," said Sergeant Morris, quickly. "At least nothing worth hearing."

"Monkey's paw?" said Mrs. White, curiously.

"Well, it's what some people might perhaps call magic," said the sergeant, thoughtfully.

His three listeners leaned forward eagerly, as the sergeant fumbled for an object in his jacket. He took something out of the pocket and showed it to them. "To look at," he said, "it's just an ordinary little paw, dried up and dirty."

Mrs. White drew back with a look of shock on her face, but Herbert took the paw and examined it curiously.

"And what is there special about this?" asked Mr. White, as he took the paw from his son and placed it on the table.

"It had a magic spell put on it by a fakir—a very holy man in India. He wanted to show that fate ruled people's lives, and that those who **interfered** with fate did so to their sorrow. He put a spell on it so that three people could have three wishes from the paw.

His manner was so serious that his listeners held back their smiles.

"Well, then, why don't *you* have three wishes, sir?" asked Herbert White.

The sergeant stared at the young man and shuddered slightly. "I have," he said quietly, and his face turned pale.

And did you really have the three wishes granted?" said Mrs. White.

"I did," said the sergeant, nodding his head slowly.

"And has anybody else wished?" asked Mrs. White.

"The first man had his three wishes, yes," was the reply. "I don't know what the first two were, but the third was for death." The sergeant paused and then added, "That's how I got the paw."

"If you've had your three wishes," said Mr. White, "the paw's no good to you now. Why do you keep it?"

The sergeant shook his head. "I did have some idea of selling it, but I don't think I will. It has caused enough trouble already. Besides, people won't buy. Some think it's all nonsense, and others want to try it first and pay me later."

"If you could have another three wishes," said Mr. White, eyeing him closely, "would you have them?"

"I don't know," said the sergeant. "I don't know."

He took the paw suddenly and hurled it into the fire. Mr. White, with a cry, stooped down and pulled it out.

"Better let it burn," said the sergeant solemnly.

"If you don't want it, Morris," said Mr. White, "give it to me."

"I won't," said his friend, stubbornly. "I threw it into the fire. If you keep it, don't blame me for what happens. Throw it on the fire again like a sensible person."

Mr. White shook his head and examined his new possession closely.

"How do you do it?" he asked.

"Just hold it up in your right hand and wish aloud," said the sergeant. "But I warn you of the **consequences**."

"It sounds like a children's story to me," said Mrs. White, as she went into the kitchen.

Her husband stared at the paw as the sergeant, with a look of alarm on his face, caught him by the arm.

"If you *must* wish," he said pointedly, "be very careful what you wish for."

They all sat down for dinner and the business about the paw was nearly forgotten. When the meal was over, the sergeant told some more tales of his adventures in India.

After their guest had left, Mrs. White asked her husband, "Did you give him anything for the paw?"

"Just a little something," he answered. "He didn't want it, but I made him take it. And he begged me again to throw the paw away."

"Why, father," said Herbert, jokingly, "we're going to be rich and famous. Wish to be a king, father. That's a good way to start."

And he and his mother marched around the table, saluting him cheerfully.

Mr. White took the paw from his pocket and eyed it questioningly.

"I don't know what to wish for, and that's a fact," he said slowly. "It seems to me I've got all I want."

"You'd be glad to pay off the house, wouldn't you," said Herbert, with his hand on his father's shoulder. "Well, wish for five hundred dollars, then. That'll just do it."

His father held up the paw as Herbert winked at his mother.

"I wish for five hundred dollars," Mr. White said very clearly.

No sooner had he finished saying these words, than a loud shuddering cry came from the father. His wife and son rushed toward him.

"It moved!" he cried, with a glance at the paw as it lay on the floor. "As I wished, it suddenly twisted in my hand like a snake!"

"Well I don't see the money," said Herbert, as he picked up the paw and placed it on the table. "And I bet we never will."

"It must have been your imagination," said Mrs. White, looking worriedly at her husband.

He shook his head. "Never mind, then," he said. "There's no harm done. Still it gave me a shock just the same."

They sat down again by the fire. Outside the wind was howling harder than ever. Mr. White jumped nervously at the sound of a door banging upstairs. An unusual silence settled on all three until the couple rose to go to bed.

"You'll probably find the cash tied up in a big bag in the middle of your bed," teased Herbert, as he said goodnight. "And some horrible creature sitting next to it who'll watch you count your unearned treasure."

A bright winter's sun shone over the breakfast table next morning. Herbert could not resist joking about what had taken place the night before.

"The idea of our listening to such nonsense," said Mrs. White, turning toward her husband. "How could wishes be granted these days? And even if they could, how could five hundred dollars hurt you?"

"Might drop on his head from out of the sky," Herbert said, laughing.

"Still," said Mr. White, "Morris seemed so serious about it all. And about bad luck always following the wishes."

"Well, don't spend all the money before I get back," said Herbert, smiling, as he rose from the table to leave for work.

Mrs. White laughed and followed him to the door. She watched him go down the road before returning to the table. And although she made light of the paw, she seemed somewhat nervous all day and rushed to the door at the slightest noise.

"I guess Herbert will have some more funny remarks to make when he comes home from work," she said as they sat at lunch.

"I suppose so," said Mr. White. "Still, say what you will, that thing moved in my hand. I'm sure of it."

"You mean you thought it moved," said his wife.

"No, I'm certain of it," he replied. "I tell you, it moved. I—why what's the matter?"

His wife did not answer. She was watching the mysterious movements of a man outside. He seemed to be making up his mind whether or not to come to the door. Three times he stopped at the gate and then

13

walked away. The fourth time he pushed it open and walked up the path. Mrs. White thought of the five hundred dollars, for she noticed that the stranger was very well dressed. She hurried to the door and asked him in.

The stranger seemed ill at ease and did not speak at once.

"I—I was asked to call," he said at last. "I come from the office of Maw and Meggins."

Mrs. White jumped. "Is anything the matter?" she asked breathlessly. "Has anything happened to Herbert? What is it? What is it?"

Her husband interrupted. "There, there," he said quickly. "Don't jump to conclusions. You've not brought bad news, I'm sure," he said to the man.

"I'm sorry—" said the visitor.

"Is Herbert hurt?" demanded the mother.

The visitor shook his head slowly. "Badly hurt," he said quietly. "But he is not in any pain."

"Thank goodness for that," said the mother. "Thank goodness—"

She broke off instantly as she suddenly realized the terrible meaning of the visitor's words. She caught her breath and turning to her husband, put her shaking hand on his.

"He was crushed in the machinery," said the visitor, finally, in a low voice.

"Crushed in the machinery," repeated Mr. White, looking dazed.

He stared blankly out the window. "He was our only son," he said softly.

The visitor coughed and walked slowly to the window. "The company wished me to offer their sincere sympathy to you in your great loss," he said. "They asked me to say that Maw and Meggins bears no **responsibility** for the accident. But in consideration of your son's service, they wish to present you with a certain sum of money."

Mr. White dropped his wife's hand and gazed with a look of horror at the visitor. "How much?" he asked.

"Five hundred dollars," was the answer.

Unaware of his wife's cry, Mr. White fell, like a senseless heap, to the floor.

In the huge new cemetery two miles away, Herbert was buried. The old couple came back to a house of shadow and silence. It had all happened so quickly they could hardly believe it, and their days were long and weary.

It was about a week after that that Mr. White awoke suddenly in the middle of the night. He stretched out his hand and found himself alone. The room was in darkness, and he heard the sound of his wife weeping near the window.

He raised himself in bed. "Come back," he said tenderly. "You will be cold."

"It is colder for our son," she answered quietly.

His eyes were heavy with sleep, and he began to **doze** when a sudden wild cry from his wife woke him with a start.

"The monkey's paw!" she cried wildly. "The monkey's paw!"

He jumped up in alarm. "What? What's the matter?"

She stumbled across the room toward him. "I want it," she said firmly. "You haven't destroyed it?"

"It's in the living room, on the shelf," he answered in a startled voice. "But why?"

She cried and laughed at the same time and bent over and kissed him.

"I just thought of it now," she said wildly. "Why didn't I think of it before? Why didn't you think of it?"

"Think of what?" he asked.

"The other two wishes," she replied quickly. "We've only had one."

"Wasn't that enough?" he demanded angrily.

"No!" she cried triumphantly. "We'll have one more. Go down and get the paw quickly, and wish that our boy were alive again."

The man sat up in bed.

"Get it," she demanded. "Get it quickly, and wish."

"Go back to bed," her husband said, uneasily. "You don't know what you are saying."

"We had the first wish granted," she said, her voice rising with excitement. "Why not the second?"

"It was a coincidence," muttered the old man.

"Go and get it and wish!" cried his wife.

Her husband struck a match and lit the candle. Then he made his way down to the living room and to the shelf. The monkey's paw was in its place, and he found it. Then he was struck by a horrible thought! The wish might

15

bring him his mutilated son—torn and crushed—before he had time to get out of the house! His head spun in terror as he made his way back to his wife.

Her face seemed changed as he entered the room. It was very pale and seemed to have a strange look on it. He was suddenly afraid of her.

"Wish!" she cried in a strong voice.

"It is foolish and wrong," he said, hesitating.

"Wish!" she repeated.

He raised his hand and said slowly, "I wish my son alive again."

The paw fell to the floor, and he looked at it in fear. Then he sank, shaking, into a chair. He watched as his wife, with burning eyes, walked to the window and raised the shades.

He sat until he became chilled with the cold, glancing now and then, at his wife who was peering through the window. After a while, the candle burned down and went out. With an enormous sense of relief that the paw had failed, he went back to bed. A few minutes later, he heard his wife returning.

Neither spoke. In the silence they listened to the ticking of the clock. A stair creaked, and the darkness pressed down upon them. After a while, the husband took the box of matches and struck one. Then he went downstairs for a candle.

At the foot of the stairs the match went out, and he stopped to light another. At the same moment, he heard a soft knock at the front door.

The match fell out of his hand. He stood still, holding his breath until he heard the knock again. Then he turned and rushed back to the room and closed the door behind him. A third knock sounded through the house.

"What's that?" cried his wife, jumping up.

"It's nothing" he said, his voice breaking. "It's—it's the wind against the roof."

His wife sat up in bed listening. A loud knock sounded through the house.

"It's Herbert!" she screamed. "It's Herbert!"

She ran to the door, but her husband caught her by the arm and held her tightly.

"What are you going to do?" he whispered hoarsely.

"It's Herbert," she cried. "I forgot that the cemetery was two miles away. Why are you holding me back? Let me go. I must open the door."

"Don't let it in!" cried the old man, shaking.

"Are you afraid of your own son?" she said, struggling. "Let me go! I'm coming, Herbert!"

There was another knock and another. The old woman broke free and ran from the room. Her husband followed her to the landing and called after her as she hurried downstairs.

He heard the chain rattle and the sound of the lower door bolt being drawn open. Then he heard his wife's voice calling to him.

"The upper bolt," she cried loudly. "Help me! I can't reach it!"

But her husband was on his hands and knees, searching wildly for the paw. If only he could find it *before the thing outside* got in!

The banging on the door echoed loudly throughout the house. Then he heard the scraping of a chair as his wife pulled it toward the door. He heard the creaking of the bolt as it moved slowly back. At that moment, he found the monkey's paw. Wildly he made his third and last wish!

The knocking suddenly stopped. He heard the door open, and a blast of cold wind blew up the staircase. A loud cry of disappointment from his wife gave him the courage to run down to her side. He rushed out to the gate and looked around. The streetlamp shone on a deserted road.

SELECTING DETAILS FROM THE STORY. Each of the following sentences helps you understand the story. Complete each sentence below by putting an *x* in the box next to the correct answer.

1. According to Sergeant Morris, the monkey's paw brought people
   - ☐ a. happiness.
   - ☐ b. luck.
   - ☐ c. trouble.

2. Mr. White's first wish was for
   - ☐ a. five hundred dollars.
   - ☐ b. the wealth of a king.
   - ☐ c. cash tied up in a bag.

3. Herbert was killed when he was
   - ☐ a. drowned in a lake.
   - ☐ b. crushed in machinery.
   - ☐ c. trapped in a fire.

4. Mrs. White demanded that her husband wish that
   - ☐ a. they had a new house.
   - ☐ b. they could travel to India.
   - ☐ c. their son were alive again.

HANDLING STORY ELEMENTS. Each of the following questions reviews your understanding of story elements. Put an *x* in the box next to the correct answer to each question.

1. What happened first in the *plot* of the story?
   - ☐ a. A stranger offered the Whites five hundred dollars.
   - ☐ b. Mrs. White pulled a chair toward the door.
   - ☐ c. Sergeant Morris threw the paw into the fire.

2. Which sentence best *characterizes* Mr. White?
   - ☐ a. He was greedy and longed to be rich.
   - ☐ b. He was unhappy because he didn't get along with his family.
   - ☐ c. He was satisfied with what he had until he obtained the monkey's paw.

3. "The Monkey's Paw" is *set* in
   - ☐ a. a factory.
   - ☐ b. a small house.
   - ☐ c. an office.

4. What is the *mood* of the story?
   - ☐ a. humorous and amusing
   - ☐ b. serious and suspenseful
   - ☐ c. happy and joyous

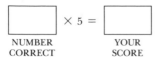

NUMBER CORRECT   × 5 =   YOUR SCORE

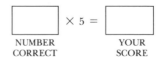

NUMBER CORRECT   × 5 =   YOUR SCORE

OBSERVING NEW VOCABULARY WORDS. Answer the following vocabulary questions by putting an *x* in the box next to the correct answer. The vocabulary words are printed in **boldface** in the story. If you wish, look back at the words before you answer the questions.

1. He began to doze, when a sudden cry from his wife woke him with a start. What is the meaning of the word *doze*?
   ☐ a. tremble
   ☐ b. think
   ☐ c. sleep

2. Although the company offered money after Herbert died, they took no responsibility for the accident. As used here, the word *responsibility* means
   ☐ a. blame.
   ☐ b. reward.
   ☐ c. grief.

3. The sergeant warned Mr. White of the consequences of making a wish. The word *consequences* means
   ☐ a. joys.
   ☐ b. results.
   ☐ c. arguments.

4. He believed that fate ruled people's lives, and those who interfered with it met with sorrow. The word *interfered* means
   ☐ a. assisted or helped.
   ☐ b. wondered about.
   ☐ c. got in the way of.

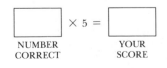

NUMBER CORRECT × 5 = YOUR SCORE

COMPLETING A CLOZE PASSAGE. Complete the following paragraph by filling in each blank with one of the words listed in the box below. Each of the words appears in the story. Since there are five words and four blanks, one word in the group will not be used.

A group of people was once asked the following ＿＿＿＿＿1＿＿＿＿＿: "What would you wish for if you could have ＿＿＿＿＿2＿＿＿＿＿ wishes?" The people were asked to write their answers on slips of paper. The papers were collected later and were read with great ＿＿＿＿＿3＿＿＿＿＿. More than half of the people wished for more than three ＿＿＿＿＿4＿＿＿＿＿.

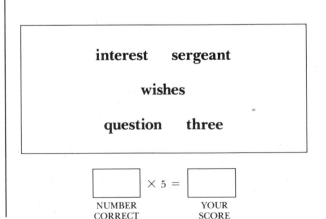

interest   sergeant

wishes

question   three

NUMBER CORRECT × 5 = YOUR SCORE

20

KNOWING HOW TO READ CRITICALLY. Each of the following questions will help you to think critically about the selection. Put an *x* in the box next to the correct answer.

1. Mr. White was afraid that his son would return and
   ☐ a. accuse him of murder.
   ☐ b. start a fight with Sergeant Morris.
   ☐ c. be terrifying to look at.

2. We may infer (figure out) that Mr. White's last wish made
   ☐ a. his wife happy.
   ☐ b. his friend, Sergeant Morris, angry.
   ☐ c. his son disappear.

3. Clues in the story suggest that the monkey's paw brought Sergeant Morris
   ☐ a. great pleasure.
   ☐ b. many treasures.
   ☐ c. unhappiness.

4. Which statement is true?
   ☐ a. When he wished, Mr. White thought that the paw twisted in his hand.
   ☐ b. Herbert was certain that the paw would make them rich.
   ☐ c. Sergeant Morris demanded that Mr. White pay him for the monkey's paw.

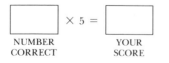

NUMBER   × 5 =   YOUR
CORRECT   SCORE

Questions for Writing and Discussion
- Sometimes a story offers a moral or lesson. What lesson or lessons can be drawn from "The Monkey's Paw"?
- What do you think Mr. White wished for at the end of the story? Provide his exact words. Suppose you were Mr. White. What would you have said?
- Suppose Mrs. White had *not* cried out in disappointment at the end of the story. Do you think Mr. White would have run to her side? Explain your answer.

Use the boxes below to total your scores for the exercises. Then write your score on pages 150 and 151.

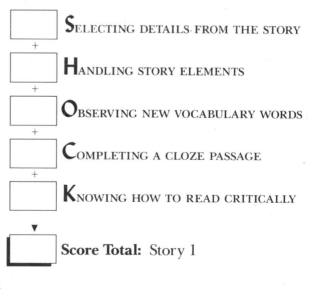

☐ **S**ELECTING DETAILS FROM THE STORY
   +
☐ **H**ANDLING STORY ELEMENTS
   +
☐ **O**BSERVING NEW VOCABULARY WORDS
   +
☐ **C**OMPLETING A CLOZE PASSAGE
   +
☐ **K**NOWING HOW TO READ CRITICALLY
   ▼
☐ **Score Total:** Story 1

2

The Love Powder

by O. Henry

The Blue Light Drug Store is downtown between the Bowery and First Avenue. The Blue Light is a very *serious* drug store. It does not sell candy or chewing gum or soda. It deals in medicines and prescriptions.

Micky Schack was the night clerk of the Blue Light and the friend of many of his customers. At the Blue Light one seeks more than mere medicine. There one asks aid and advice and assistance. And Micky's words of wisdom were warmly welcomed.

Micky lived and ate dinners at Mrs. Riddle's boardinghouse two blocks away. Mrs. Riddle had a daughter named Rosy and—as you must have guessed—Micky **adored** her. To him she was the sun and the moon—and all the stars in the heavens.

But Micky was timid, and his hopes remained frozen in fear. Behind his counter he was confident and calm, the master of his trade. Away from the store he was weak-kneed and hesitant. Faint-hearted and shy, he lacked the courage to tell Rosy.

To add to his problem there was Chunk McGowan. Chunk also roomed at the Riddle's and was crazy about Rosy. At the same time he was Micky's friend and customer and often dropped in at the Blue Light to have a cut or bruise treated after a playful sidewalk scuffle.

One afternoon McGowan drifted in in his easy way, and sat, good-natured, upon a stool.

"Micky," he said to his friend behind the counter, "there's an item I need—if you can make it for me."

Micky stared at Chunk's face, searching hard for the signs of the usual wounds. "Where's the injury?" he asked.

Mr. McGowan smiled. "The trouble," he said, "has to do with my *heart.* Say Micky—Rosy and me are going to run away and get married tonight."

Micky's eyes opened wide.

"That is," continued Chunk, the smile fading from his face, "if she doesn't change her mind before the time comes. We've been making plans for the great event for the past two weeks. One day she says she will. The same evening she says no. We've agreed on tonight. And Rosy's stuck to that for two days in a row. But there are still five hours to go—and I'm afraid that she'll back out at the very last minute."

"You said there was an item you needed from me," remarked Micky slowly.

Mr. McGowan looked ill at ease, a condition quite unusual for him.

"I wouldn't have this foul up for anything in the world," he went on. "I've rented a little apartment uptown, with flowers on the table and a kettle ready to boil. And I've hired a preacher to marry us at his house at 9:30 sharp. Our plan's got to work! And it will!—if Rosy doesn't change her mind again." Mr. McGowan shook his head sadly, troubled by his doubts.

"I still don't see yet," said Micky shortly, "what it is that you want of me, or what I can be doing about that."

"Old man Riddle don't like me at all," McGowan continued. "For a week now he hasn't let Rosy step outside the door with me. If they could afford to lose a boarder, they'd have bounced me out a long time ago. I think the world of her, and she'll never regret flyin' the coop with Chunk McGowan."

"You will excuse me, Chunk," said Micky. "I must make up something that is to be picked up soon."

"Say," said McGowan, looking up suddenly. "Say, Micky, isn't there some kind of powder—a love powder, you know, that'll make a girl like you better if you give it to her?"

Micky's lip curled with scorn at this foolish idea. But before he could answer, Chunk went on. "Yes, a love powder, Micky, that's what I need."

Strong and simple was Chunk McGowan. A better judge of men than

Micky was would have seen that Chunk's tough frame was strung on delicate wires. Like a good general in foreign territory, he was trying to guard every path against possible failure.

"I thought," went on Chunk, hopefully, "that if I had one of them love powders to give Rosy when I see her at supper tonight, it might brace her up a bit. You know, keep her from backing out on our plan to skip. I guess she doesn't need a team of mules to drag her away. But I'd like to make sure. If the stuff works for a couple of hours, it'll do the trick."

"When is this foolishness of running away supposed to happen?" asked Micky.

"Nine o'clock," said Mr. McGowan. "Supper's at seven. At eight Rosy says she has a bad headache and goes to bed. At nine I slip into Riddle's backyard through the space where there's a board off his fence. I go under Rosy's window and help her down the fire escape. It's got to go off like clockwork so we can get to the preacher on time. It's all dead easy if Rosy doesn't back out. Can you fix me one of them love powders, Micky?"

Micky shook his head thoughtfully.

"Chunk," said he, "it is with drugs of that nature that a druggist must take the greatest of care. To you alone of all my **acquaintances** would I trust a powder such as the one you ask. But for you I shall make it, and you shall see the power it has."

Micky went behind the counter. There he crushed to a powder a tiny tablet of morphine. To that he added a little sugar to increase the bulk. Then he folded the mixture neatly in a white paper. Taken by an adult, this powder would produce several hours of deep sleep without danger to the sleeper.

This he handed to Chunk McGowan, telling him to use it in a liquid if possible. McGowan offered his hearty thanks and **departed** with his treasure.

How very clever was Micky's plan. For no sooner had Chunk left then the druggist reached for the telephone.

He quickly informed Mr. Riddle of Chunk's plan for **eloping** with Rosy. Mr. Riddle was a man with a very quick temper.

"Much obliged," he said briefly to Micky. "We'll just see about Chunk McGowan! My room's right above Rosy's. I'll go up there after supper and load the shotgun and wait. If he comes in my backyard, he'll go away looking for a doctor instead of a preacher."

With Rosy deep in sleep and her angry parent waiting and armed, Micky felt sure that Chunk McGowan soon would be out of the picture.

All night in the Blue Light Drug Store, Micky waited for some news of the disaster. But no news came.

At eight o'clock in the morning the day clerk arrived, and Micky started hurriedly for Mrs. Riddle's to learn the outcome. Just as he stepped out of the store, who but Chunk McGowan sprang across the street and grasped his hand—Chunk McGowan with a smile of victory and bursting with joy.

"Went off without a hitch!" said Chunk with an enormous grin. "Rosy hit the fire escape on time to the second, and we made it to the preacher's at 9:30 on the nose. She's up at the apartment now. We had eggs this morning. How lucky I am! You must drop by some day and have dinner with us, Micky. I've got a job down near the bridge, and that's where I'm heading for now."

"The—the—love powder?" stammered Micky.

"Oh, that stuff you gave me," said Chunk, his grin growing even wider. "Well, it was this way. I sat down at the supper table last night at Riddle's. And I looked at Rosy and I said to myself, 'Chunk, if you're going to marry Rosy, do it fair and square. Don't try any nonsense with a gem like her.' So I kept the powder you gave me in my pocket. And then my eyes fell on another person present, someone who could show a little more affection to his future son-in-law. So I watched for my chance and dumped that love powder in old man Riddle's coffee—see?"

SELECTING DETAILS FROM THE STORY.
Each of the following sentences helps you understand the story. Complete each sentence below by putting an *x* in the box next to the correct answer.

1. Chunk was afraid that Rosy might
   ☐ a. tell her father about their plan.
   ☐ b. fall in love with Micky.
   ☐ c. change her mind about running away.

2. Chunk hoped that Micky could make him
   ☐ a. a sleeping pill.
   ☐ b. a love powder.
   ☐ c. some medicine.

3. Micky called Mr. Riddle in order to
   ☐ a. tell him about Chunk's plan.
   ☐ b. get his permission to go out with Rosy.
   ☐ c. ask to speak to Rosy.

4. At the end of the story Chunk told Micky that
   ☐ a. Rosy decided not to get married after all.
   ☐ b. Mr. Riddle had been waiting with his shotgun.
   ☐ c. the plan worked perfectly.

HANDLING STORY ELEMENTS. Each of the following questions reviews your understanding of story elements. Put an *x* in the box next to the correct answer to each question.

1. What happened last in the *plot* of the story?
   ☐ a. Chunk said that he put the love powder in Mr. Riddle's coffee.
   ☐ b. Micky made a telephone call to Mr. Riddle.
   ☐ c. Chunk told Micky that he planned to marry Rosy.

2. Which sentence best *characterizes* Micky?
   ☐ a. He was confident and bold at all times.
   ☐ b. When he was away from his store, he was timid and shy.
   ☐ c. His customers did not like him or respect him.

3. "The Love Powder" is *set* in
   ☐ a. a drugstore.
   ☐ b. a backyard.
   ☐ c. an apartment uptown.

4. Which sentence best tells the *theme* of the story?
   ☐ a. It is wise to be honest with the person you love.
   ☐ b. It is not really possible to make a love powder.
   ☐ c. A druggist tries to ruin a friend's plan, but he ends up helping him.

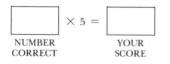

NUMBER CORRECT × 5 = YOUR SCORE

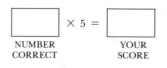

NUMBER CORRECT × 5 = YOUR SCORE

OBSERVING NEW VOCABULARY WORDS. Answer the following vocabulary questions by putting an *x* in the box next to the correct answer. The vocabulary words are printed in **boldface** in the story. If you wish, look back at the words before you answer the questions.

1. Micky adored Rosy: to him she was the sun and the moon, and all the stars in the heavens. The word *adored* means
   ☐ a. avoided.
   ☐ b. was jealous of.
   ☐ c. loved greatly.

2. Chunk McGowan took the love powder, offered his thanks, and departed with his treasure. The word *departed* means
   ☐ a. went away.
   ☐ b. stared at.
   ☐ c. forgot.

3. Although Micky had many customers, Chunk was the only one of his acquaintances he would trust with a love powder. What are *acquaintances*?
   ☐ a. people one knows casually
   ☐ b. people one never sees
   ☐ c. people one doesn't like

4. Micky told Mr. Riddle about Chunk's plan for eloping with Rosy. The word *eloping* means
   ☐ a. borrowing money from.
   ☐ b. running away to get married.
   ☐ c. telling lies to.

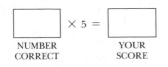

NUMBER
CORRECT

YOUR
SCORE

COMPLETING A CLOZE PASSAGE. Complete the following paragraph by filling in each blank with one of the words listed in the box below. Each of the words appears in the story. Since there are five words and four blanks, one word in the group will not be used.

How much sleep a person

_____ really depends upon
         1

that person. Studies show that most adults

_____ seven to eight hours a
         2

night. However, some people can get along

quite well with just a _____ of
                              3

hours of sleep, while other people must

sleep ten to twelve hours a night. It is not

_____ to say exactly how much
         4

sleep a person should have.

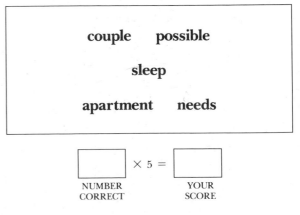

couple	possible
sleep	
apartment	needs

NUMBER
CORRECT

YOUR
SCORE

28

KNOWING HOW TO READ CRITICALLY. Each of the following questions will help you to think critically about the selection. Put an *x* in the box next to the correct answer.

1. Why didn't Mr. Riddle chase Chunk away at nine o'clock that evening?
   - ☐ a. He changed his mind about Chunk.
   - ☐ b. He forgot all about Chunk's plan.
   - ☐ c. He was sound asleep.

2. Chunk put the powder in Mr. Riddle's coffee because he
   - ☐ a. wanted Mr. Riddle to like him better.
   - ☐ b. didn't have a chance to put it in Rosy's drink.
   - ☐ c. knew that it would put Mr. Riddle to sleep.

3. Chunk told Micky that he had trouble that had "to do with my heart." By this Chunk meant that he
   - ☐ a. had been ill for years with a heart disease.
   - ☐ b. had a problem that had to do with love.
   - ☐ c. needed to see a doctor at once.

4. At the end of the story, Micky probably felt
   - ☐ a. pleased.
   - ☐ b. shocked.
   - ☐ c. amused.

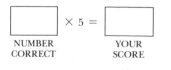

NUMBER
CORRECT

× 5 =

YOUR
SCORE

Questions for Writing and Discussion

- After he called Mr. Riddle, Micky waited all night for "news of the disaster." What did Micky expect to hear when he arrived at Mrs. Riddle's boardinghouse? Describe that scene as vividly as possible.
- The author states that "Chunk's tough frame was strung on delicate wires." What does that mean?
- Micky asked Chunk, "When is this foolishness of running away supposed to happen?" Should that remark have made Chunk suspicious? Give reasons for your answer.

Use the boxes below to total your scores for the exercises. Then write your score on pages 150 and 151.

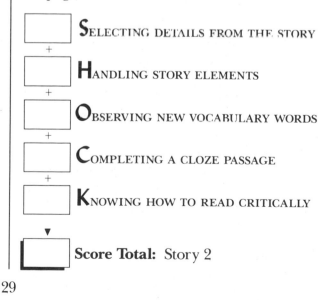

SELECTING DETAILS FROM THE STORY

+

HANDLING STORY ELEMENTS

+

OBSERVING NEW VOCABULARY WORDS

+

COMPLETING A CLOZE PASSAGE

+

KNOWING HOW TO READ CRITICALLY

▼

Score Total: Story 2

3

Dear Amanda

by Linnah Gary

*A*manda sat moodily on her bed, gazing silently around the room. Her glance fell upon her ancient desk. It had seen every act, had heard every thought expressed in the privacy and quiet of that dim attic room. Amanda noticed the bottom drawer of the desk sticking out. It looked like the **pouting** lip of an angry child. She got up and wandered slowly across the room, intending to close the drawer.

As she neared the old desk, Amanda suddenly remembered something. She quickened her pace. Then she yanked open the stubborn drawer. Inside Amanda found the package of letters. It was tied with a piece of worn blue ribbon. Carefully she lifted the **fragile** pages from the mess of erasers, pencils, and old school papers. Then she worked impatiently at untying the tight knot.

Amanda raised her head for a moment. As she did, she caught her reflection in the dusty mirror above the dresser right next to her bed. She noted with interest the unusual glitter in her gray eyes. She saw a spot of color in her pale cheeks.

Amanda looked closely at the lifeless brown hair which hung about her face. What was wrong with it? she wondered. Unhappy with what she saw, she turned her attention to the bundle of letters clutched tightly in her hands. Settling herself in the chair at the desk, she switched on the bulb overhead. She wondered which letter to read first.

She chose one written on pale blue notepaper. Deep folds wrinkled its once smooth surface. A blurry spot marred the handwriting on the second page. Amanda unfolded the sheets which were no longer crisp. She began to read:

Dear Amanda,

I just got home from practice, and thought I'd write you a letter. I can't talk to those guys on the team. You're the only one who listens and understands. It's great to have a girl who listens the way you do.

We studied poetry today in school. I really like the stuff, but we have to write some of our own for next week. You know for sure I'm no star when it comes to being creative, Mandy. I haven't got the talent you have for writing. You write such beautiful poetry, you ought to **submit** it to a magazine or something. I really mean it. Maybe you could give me a few tips. I'm so lost, and I'm positive you could help, since you . . .

Amanda read on eagerly, losing herself in the precious letters. Uneasily, she remembered how her mother had scolded her about shutting herself up in her room to read. She knew her mother must think it silly for her to even get letters. The thought hurt Amanda, and she comforted herself by saying her mother just didn't understand. Maybe that was why she was always so cross. Amanda felt sure that was the reason.

One letter in particular Amanda loved. It was by far the most worn of

the collection. She opened it and held it closer to the light so that she could see the faded writing more clearly.

My dearest Amanda,

It has been a long time since I have written you. Please forgive me, won't you? I know you will. You are such a kind person.

My sister dragged me along to go shopping with her last week. She asked me to help her pick out some clothes. I certainly wish that you had been along. I don't know much about girls' styles. You have such good taste. Things always look perfect on you. Sis finally picked out a blue dress. I couldn't help thinking how nice it would have looked with your hair. Really, Mandy, I think that you . . .

Amanda loved those lines. At least someone thought that she looked pretty. Her mother always complained about how sloppy Amanda looked.

"Amanda, you're not going to wear that dress, are you?" she always said. "It doesn't do a thing for you. Amanda, I wish you'd do something with your hair. Amanda, for goodness sake, straighten up. Amanda, why don't you try to look a little more pleasant?"

On and on she went that way, until Amanda angrily rushed back to her room. She told herself that her mother didn't really know what she was talking about.

A sharp voice **jolted** Amanda from her deep thoughts.

"Amanda! Just exactly what are you doing up there? I've been calling you for the last fifteen minutes. I want you to come down here immediately. Do you hear me? Amanda?"

Amanda didn't answer. She didn't want to break the wonderful spell of the letters. Then, hearing loud footsteps on the stairs, she quickly shuffled together the sheets of wrinkled paper. Her mother burst into the room. An angry expression clouded her face.

"Amanda! I thought I told you to get rid of those silly things. Give them to me. And get yourself downstairs, young lady, or your father will hear of this!"

Amanda slammed the door at her mother's back and stomped furiously back to her desk. Fumbling and angry, she searched frantically for paper and pen. Then she seated herself and began to write.

Dear Amanda,
    I've got to write to you. You're so . . .

SELECTING DETAILS FROM THE STORY.
Each of the following sentences helps
you understand the story. Complete each
sentence below by putting an *x* in the
box next to the correct answer.

1. When Amanda saw her reflection in
   the mirror, she
   ☐ a. was satisfied with what she saw.
   ☐ b. didn't like the way she looked.
   ☐ c. wished that her eyes were not
   gray.

2. The letter that Amanda loved best said
   that she
   ☐ a. had very good taste.
   ☐ b. was an excellent athlete.
   ☐ c. was probably the smartest person
   in school.

3. According to Amanda, her mother
   always complained about
   ☐ a. Amanda's friends.
   ☐ b. Amanda's classmates.
   ☐ c. how sloppy Amanda looked.

4. At the end of the story, Amanda
   ☐ a. reached for paper and pen and
   began to write.
   ☐ b. rushed downstairs at once.
   ☐ c. gave her mother the letters.

HANDLING STORY ELEMENTS. Each of
the following questions reviews your
understanding of story elements. Put
an *x* in the box next to the correct
answer to each question.

1. Where is "Dear Amanda" *set*?
   ☐ a. in an attic
   ☐ b. at the library
   ☐ c. at school

2. What happened first in the *plot* of
   "Dear Amanda"?
   ☐ a. Amanda slammed the door and
   stomped back to her desk.
   ☐ b. Amanda's mother demanded
   that Amanda come downstairs
   at once.
   ☐ c. Amanda opened the drawer and
   found the package of letters.

3. Which word best *characterizes* Amanda?
   ☐ a. popular
   ☐ b. unhappy
   ☐ c. cheerful

4. In this story, there is *conflict* between
   ☐ a. Amanda's mother and father.
   ☐ b. Amanda and someone who was
   writing letters to her.
   ☐ c. Amanda and her mother.

☐ × 5 = ☐
NUMBER   YOUR
CORRECT SCORE

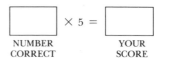

☐ × 5 = ☐
NUMBER   YOUR
CORRECT SCORE

OBSERVING NEW VOCABULARY WORDS. Answer the following vocabulary questions by putting an *x* in the box next to the correct answer. The vocabulary words are printed in **boldface** in the story. If you wish, look back at the words before you answer the questions.

1. Amanda carefully lifted the fragile pages from the mess of old school papers. The word *fragile* means
   □ a. large.
   □ b. sturdy.
   □ c. easily broken.

2. The drawer stuck out like the pouting lip of an angry child. A lip that is *pouting* is
   □ a. injured.
   □ b. pushed out unhappily.
   □ c. very thin.

3. The letter suggested that Amanda submit her poetry to a magazine. As used here, the word *submit* means
   □ a. send or offer.
   □ b. purchase or buy.
   □ c. read or recite.

4. A sharp voice jolted Amanda from her deep thoughts. What is the meaning of the word *jolted*?
   □ a. shocked
   □ b. soothed
   □ c. pleased

COMPLETING A CLOZE PASSAGE. Complete the following paragraph by filling in each blank with one of the words listed in the box below. Each of the words appears in the story. Since there are five words and four blanks, one word in the group will not be used.

   "Dear Amanda" was written by Linnah

Gary when she was still a student in

high _____. Linnah's English

teacher thought that Linnah's writing

showed _____. He advised her
                2

to send the story to a _____.
                                3

It was published there, won an award,

and has appeared in several short story

_____.
        4

| talent   school |
| magazine |
| beautiful   collections |

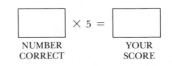

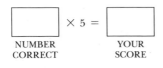

KNOWING HOW TO READ CRITICALLY. Each of the following questions will help you to think critically about the selection. Put an *x* in the box next to the correct answer.

1. We may infer (figure out) that the letters to Amanda were written by
   ☐ a. Amanda's friends.
   ☐ b. Amanda's classmates.
   ☐ c. Amanda herself.

2. Which statement is true?
   ☐ a. Amanda usually got tired of reading the letters.
   ☐ b. Writing and reading the letters made Amanda feel better about herself.
   ☐ c. Amanda thought that most of the letters were very boring.

3. Clues in the story suggest that Amanda
   ☐ a. didn't think she was pretty.
   ☐ b. thought she was beautiful.
   ☐ c. almost never got angry.

4. A "blurry spot marred the handwriting" on the page of one wrinkled letter. This spot was probably caused by a
   ☐ a. tear.
   ☐ b. raindrop.
   ☐ c. glass of water.

Questions for Writing and Discussion
- One letter stated that Amanda was creative and had a talent for writing. Do you agree with that opinion? Explain your answer.
- Suppose you could offer some words of advice to Amanda. What would you tell her?
- The author wrote "Dear Amanda" when she was 17 years old. Does that surprise you? Why?

Use the boxes below to total your scores for the exercises. Then write your score on pages 150 and 151.

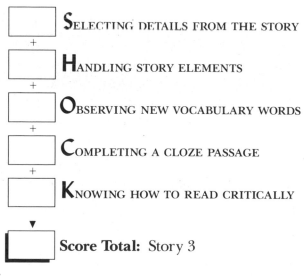

☐ **S**ELECTING DETAILS FROM THE STORY

+

☐ **H**ANDLING STORY ELEMENTS

+

☐ **O**BSERVING NEW VOCABULARY WORDS

+

☐ **C**OMPLETING A CLOZE PASSAGE

+

☐ **K**NOWING HOW TO READ CRITICALLY

▼

☐ **Score Total:** Story 3

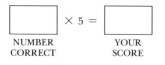

☐ × 5 = ☐

NUMBER   YOUR
CORRECT   SCORE

4

The Expression

by José Francés

A few minutes before the curtain went up, the theater manager knocked on the door of Pablo Heredia's dressing room.

"Heredia, may I come in?" he asked.

"Come in, Luis."

Heredia, the star actor, turned his gaze away from the looking glass and faced the manager.

"What's the matter, Luis? Why so gloomy? Small audience again?"

"Yes," Luis said, frowning. "So small that we cannot go on like this. We *must* put on the other play, *The Criminals*. We must do it at once! Or there will be no money for salaries next month." He dropped heavily into an armchair near the dressing table, sighing loudly as he did.

Heredia did not answer. He turned his attention to the looking glass and continued to put on his makeup.

There was a long silence. Neither man wanted to speak first. Each was afraid he might say the wrong thing.

The manager had great faith in *The Criminals*. It was a rough and powerful work about crime. Three months ago he had eagerly suggested it to Heredia. With the great actor in the main role, the manager was convinced it would be a big hit.

At that time, Heredia **enthusiastically** accepted the play. He agreed it would be his greatest triumph yet. But during practices, Heredia had trouble with the final scene. In it the character he plays receives a knife wound and lies dying, from loss of blood, at the feet of a woman.

In those rehearsals Heredia played the scene with a certain expression on his face. But it was an expression which was not moving enough, not quite—*right*. The theater manager said that he was not concerned. He was sure that when the play opened to the public, Heredia's face would perfectly **display** the expression that the moment required. Yes, everyone was convinced of this. The actors and all the members of the company said so.

At first, Heredia was proud of their confidence. But after a while he began to feel a sense of fear, of *dread,* about that final scene. What should the expression on his face be like? It must show rage and pain and love and shame at his defeat—and show them all at once! What should the eyes be like? Should his face grow pale? How should the voice sound? And should his hands tremble? Should they claw the air? Or should he **clench** his fists?

These were difficult questions, questions to which he could find no answer. Day after day Heredia stood in front of the looking glass, practicing. But still he was not satisfied. He could not get the expression right. He thought about it all day. It kept him awake at night.

On and on the practices went, as Heredia put off the opening date. All the actors knew their parts by heart. Still Heredia delayed and postponed the opening.

Now, in the dressing room, Luis, the manager, rose from the armchair. "Heredia," he said in a sharp voice, "we cannot continue this way! We must put on *The Criminals* at once. We must set a date. There is no other way!"

Heredia did not answer at first. But then, unhappily, he agreed. "All right," he said, uneasily. "Let's say two weeks from today. We'll make that the opening night."

"Two weeks!" exclaimed Luis. "No, Heredia, certainly not. Today is Monday. The play must go on Friday. That will give us four full houses for sure—opening night on Friday, Saturday evening, and two shows on Sunday. Three days are enough to prepare. You arrange for the final rehearsals. I'll tell the newspapers and the photographers. Then I'll order posters and tickets from the printers. Do you agree?"

Heredia did not answer.

"Heredia, do you agree?"

"Very well," Heredia replied slowly. "I agree."

About two o'clock in the morning, Heredia left the theater alone. The night was damp and misty, and the chill in the air made him turn up his coat.

He walked about aimlessly, eager to be alone, to think. He was concerned, worried—and a bit frightened. He had made an important decision, one which would permit salaries to be paid. And yet—that final scene. How should his face express that terrible moment? What should his eyes be like? Should he grow pale?

He walked along deaf to everything around him. He did not even feel the steady drizzle. All he knew was that opening night was just three days away.

Gradually he left the wide main avenues and entered the poorer sections; streets of crime and poverty, with lamps that shone yellow.

Suddenly he stopped and looked around him. He had lost his way. He was at the far end of a narrow street. To the left, the darkness of vacant land. To the right, unfriendly buildings with narrow doorways.

Not a voice. No sound of footsteps. He started walking back quickly, telling himself he was not afraid. For a moment the awful silence chilled his heart.

Where could he be? He turned a corner and stopped to look down the street. He did not recognize it and continued, more lost than ever, walking down street after street. All were unfamiliar. He grew more and more anxious. His mouth grew dry, and his temples throbbed.

By chance he found himself outside an inn. He opened the door. Heavy, evil-smelling air struck him in the face. He looked in. The room was small and dirty. There were three tables **occupied** and one empty. Behind the counter a fat man was reading a paper.

His entry created much surprise. When he sat down and unbuttoned his fur coat, there were whispers. At one table a man and a woman spoke in low tones. At a table in the corner, two men watched him closely.

He ordered something to drink. Then he realized how foolish he had been to enter there, to take off his gloves and let them see the jewels on his hands. But there was nothing he could do about that now. So, as he had done at other times of danger, he acted boldly. He stared straight at the two men in the corner. They avoided his gaze, looking away.

Slowly the actor's fears turned to curiosity. Either of those two men, he thought, could serve as the model for his character in *The Criminals*. They were poorly dressed and might have spent time in jail. But after a brief time, the two men, seeing that they were watched, exchanged a few whispered words, then left.

Time passed. Heredia got up, paid, and went out into the street. The cold and mist awaited him as before. He looked up and down, wondering which direction to take.

Well, it didn't matter. He would come out somewhere. The street was silent and deserted. His steps echoed on the pavement.

Long and narrow streets. Short and narrow streets. Suddenly, a wide avenue with trees, and black factory buildings at the end. He stopped and looked in vain for the lights of a cab.

He heard footsteps behind him. He turned and thought he saw two men in the mist. Could they be . . . ?

Heredia continued walking. Suddenly two arms seized him from behind. Someone gave him a push, and he fell forward.

Then a blow to the chest, a sharp, cold pain in his side, and he passed out.

When he opened his eyes, they were putting him on a bed in the hospital. He felt a terrible throbbing in his side. His throat was dry, his chest was pounding, his forehead damp. And he felt tired, very tired.

Vaguely he remembered seeing a knife thrust at him, perhaps death . . .

He also remembered the other thing—the expression. And suddenly, as if insane, he sat up in bed shouting. "Here! Here!" he yelled wildly. "A mirror! Quickly, bring me a mirror! I want to see my face!"

SELECTING DETAILS FROM THE STORY.
Each of the following sentences helps
you understand the story. Complete each
sentence below by putting an *x* in the
box next to the correct answer.

1. The theater manager was convinced
that the play, *The Criminals,* would
☐ a. close in a few weeks.
☐ b. be fairly successful.
☐ c. be a big hit.

2. Heredia kept putting off the opening
of the play because
☐ a. the manager refused to increase
his salary.
☐ b. he was having trouble with the
final scene.
☐ c. he didn't think the other actors
were ready.

3. At the inn, Heredia acted foolishly
when he
☐ a. let the people there see the jewels
on his hands.
☐ b. stared boldly at two men sitting
in the corner.
☐ c. ordered something to eat.

4. When he was at the hospital, Heredia
demanded that
☐ a. his attackers be found
immediately.
☐ b. his wounds be treated without
delay.
☐ c. he be given a mirror at once.

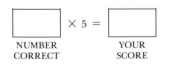

NUMBER
CORRECT   × 5 =   YOUR
SCORE

HANDLING STORY ELEMENTS. Each of
the following questions reviews your
understanding of story elements. Put
an *x* in the box next to the correct
answer to each question.

1. What happened last in the *plot* of
"The Expression"?
☐ a. Heredia entered the inn and sat
down at a table.
☐ b. Heredia felt a sharp, cold pain
in his side.
☐ c. Luis demanded that the play
open on Friday.

2. Which sentence best *characterizes* Heredia?
☐ a. He was a poor actor who did not
take his work seriously.
☐ b. He was a great actor who was
nervous about a difficult scene.
☐ c. He was selfish and did not care
if the other actors got paid.

3. "I want to see my face!" This line of
dialogue was spoken by
☐ a. Heredia.
☐ b. Luis.
☐ c. one of the attackers.

4. Which sentence best tells the *theme* of
the story?
☐ a. It is not wise to travel in a strange
neighborhood late at night.
☐ b. The life of an actor is harder
than most people realize.
☐ c. A dangerous experience provides
the answer to an actor's problem.

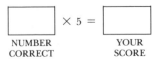

NUMBER
CORRECT   × 5 =   YOUR
SCORE

OBSERVING NEW VOCABULARY WORDS. Answer the following vocabulary questions by putting an *x* in the box next to the correct answer. The vocabulary words are printed in **boldface** in the story. If you wish, look back at the words before you answer the questions.

1. At first Heredia enthusiastically agreed to play the part, for he thought it would be his greatest triumph yet. The word *enthusiastically* means
   ☐ a. eagerly.
   ☐ b. sadly.
   ☐ c. slowly.

2. Everyone was sure that Heredia's face would display the expression that was needed. As used here, the word *display* means
   ☐ a. remove or take off.
   ☐ b. put on or show.
   ☐ c. forget or fail to remember.

3. At the inn three tables were occupied and one was empty. What is the meaning of the word *occupied*?
   ☐ a. broken
   ☐ b. solid
   ☐ c. filled

4. Heredia wondered: Should his hands tremble, or should he clench his fists? The word *clench* means
   ☐ a. close tightly together.
   ☐ b. wreck or destroy.
   ☐ c. push firmly or shove.

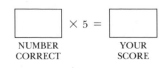

NUMBER CORRECT   YOUR SCORE

COMPLETING A CLOZE PASSAGE. Complete the following paragraph by filling in each blank with one of the words listed in the box below. Each of the words appears in the story. Since there are five words and four blanks, one word in the group will not be used.

William Shakespeare once wrote, "All the world's a stage, and all the _____ and women merely
₁

players." Perhaps Shakespeare meant that life is like a _____ . When we
₂

are born, the _____ rises. We
₃

act our parts upon the stage. Then all too soon the _____ curtain
₄

falls and we are gone. The play is over.

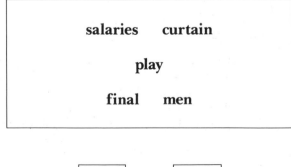

salaries   curtain

play

final   men

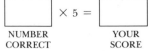

NUMBER CORRECT   YOUR SCORE

44

KNOWING HOW TO READ CRITICALLY. Each of the following questions will help you to think critically about the selection. Put an *x* in the box next to the correct answer.

1. At the end of the story, why was Heredia eager to look at his face?
   - ☐ a. He wanted to see if he had been cut.
   - ☐ b. He was concerned about his good looks.
   - ☐ c. He wanted to study his expression.

2. Heredia was probably attacked by
   - ☐ a. someone who happened to notice him on the street.
   - ☐ b. some actors who followed him out of the theater.
   - ☐ c. the two men who saw him at the inn.

3. Which statement is true?
   - ☐ a. Luis did not have confidence in Heredia's acting ability.
   - ☐ b. Heredia was very pleased that the play was to open in three days.
   - ☐ c. When Heredia left the theater, he was still concerned about the opening of the play.

4. Clues in the story suggest that Heredia was attacked because he
   - ☐ a. was thought to have money and valuables.
   - ☐ b. had made many enemies over the years.
   - ☐ c. insulted someone at the inn.

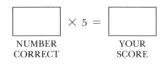

☐ × 5 = ☐

NUMBER CORRECT   YOUR SCORE

Questions for Writing and Discussion
- Compare the attack on Heredia with the final scene of *The Criminals*. In what ways are they similar?
- Think about your answer to the question above. Then explain how Heredia planned to turn the attack on him into a learning experience.
- It is obvious why this story is called "The Expression." Think of another interesting and fitting title.

Use the boxes below to total your scores for the exercises. Then write your score on pages 150 and 151.

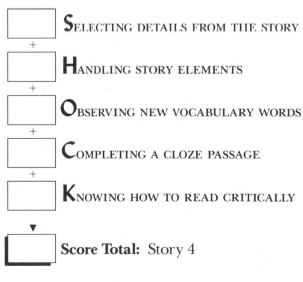

☐   **S**ELECTING DETAILS FROM THE STORY
 +
☐   **H**ANDLING STORY ELEMENTS
 +
☐   **O**BSERVING NEW VOCABULARY WORDS
 +
☐   **C**OMPLETING A CLOZE PASSAGE
 +
☐   **K**NOWING HOW TO READ CRITICALLY
 ▼
☐   **Score Total:** Story 4

5

The Cog

by Charles E. Fritch

The huge crowd arrived early in the day and had been waiting for hours. On the enormous green lawn families sat packed together, eating sandwiches and sipping soft drinks. Their voices buzzed with excitement like thousands of bees.

High above, the sun glinted off the shiny metal of the spaceship, *President.* The craft towered in the sky like a silver needle, casting a long, dark shadow on the people below.

James Maxwell sat and listened to the hum of the voices. Maxwell knew what had brought so many people here. Some were curious. A few were scientists. Others wished to be present at this important event. But many **spectators**, especially the younger ones, were here simply because they felt the urge—the powerful *longing* to travel in space far beyond the stars.

Longing? Maxwell wondered if anyone had ever felt that longing as deeply as he had. But at the same time, he knew that they had. People had

always felt the call of the stars. In his heart he was sure that they always would.

Maxwell felt a touch of regret as he wondered how many of the youngsters here would succeed in their wish to reach the stars. And how many, many more would fail, as *he* had failed. They would take the sensible, respectable jobs in the community. They would become cogs in the machinery of society.

And yet society needed cogs to make the wheels of its machinery run. Everyone couldn't be an astronaut, of course. The world needed doctors, and teachers, and even government officials. *Everyone* was a cog—from the President down to the lowest-paid worker. Even the astronauts were cogs— all cogs in the machine.

Yes, *even the astronauts were cogs,* he thought to himself.

And then, suddenly, he wasn't so sure. He stared into the bright afternoon sky and wondered, as he often did. And he asked himself the same old question: What would have happened if he had followed Gerald Adams' path twenty years ago?

He and Gerald had shared the longing, the call of the stars. Gerald, too, had stared out into the cool blackness of the night. But Gerald had seen and found his future there.

Gerald Adams had been the first astronaut to land on Venus.

Later, he had died in space, touching down on Mars. His rocket had broken apart, bursting into a million **fragments**. Still, Gerald had achieved his dream. To die in space was his destiny—and he would not have changed it for anything.

James Maxwell wondered how *he* would die. In bed, probably, an old man—too **feeble** to make it to the next room, much less to the stars!

Sometimes he felt that fate had played a cruel joke on him. But there it was and what could he do? The answer was the same as always: nothing.

"Maybe next year," he'd told Gerald. James Maxwell had gone to law school. His family was so practical, so very practical.

"Do the **sensible** thing," they'd said. Then, when his chance had passed him by, he'd felt cheated. He wanted to blame others—but nobody else was really to blame. Now he waited quietly staring up at the sky. He had no excuses to offer.

A speaker appeared and the crowd suddenly hushed. The voice boomed out over the loudspeaker. It swept over the huge crowd, while the great spaceship sparkled and shone in the late afternoon sun.

The man spoke of the glorious conquest of space—of the women and men who had led the way—of the women and men who would journey today among the stars.

James Maxwell let his gaze wander upward. He stared at the shining metal spaceship. In less than an hour the crowd would be asked to move back. Then they'd watch with pounding hearts as the powerful rocket roared into the sky. James Maxwell could feel his own heart beating faster. Very soon, he knew, the rocket would be knifing through space, speeding toward the light of Alpha Centauri.

If only he were aboard that rocket!

The feeling was still there. If only he could leave the life he had now. If only he could trade it for that of a crew member. If only—

He nearly laughed aloud. It was too late, years too late. Others would be aboard the *President*—younger people, people who had been trained to do their job, trained to be cogs that helped run the machine.

James Maxwell was a cog, too. He had studied law. He had also been trained. The machine had found a place for him. It's that simple, he thought.

The crowd suddenly cheered again, as the crew of the *President* came onto the speaker's stand. The astronauts shifted nervously, smiling, proud of the part they would play, these pleased but humble voyagers in the vastness of space.

James Maxwell looked carefully at each face. He could read his thoughts there. How he wished he could go with them! He felt a sudden stab of jealousy, but he was not bitter. This was the way it was, the way it had to be.

A great cheer went up as Mercedes Diaz, Director of Space Exploration, rose and walked across the platform. She carried a pair of scissors to cut

49

the bright red ribbon in front of the spaceship. As she did, the crowd shouted and clapped and roared and cheered. The glad sounds echoed again and again in the warm afternoon air.

James Maxwell felt a part of the enthusiasm. His blood rushed through his body. His heart pounded with excitement. These people—many of them—wanted to go. But they would go in spirit only, represented by those aboard. And *they* were satisfied.

Suddenly James Maxwell realized that he, too, was satisfied. He would be represented even more than the others. In a way, it would be as though he, himself, were soaring through the depths of space.

A voice came booming over the loudspeaker. "Ladies and gentlemen . . . The President of the World Republic!"

The voice echoed from the spaceship and rolled over the crowd. As a new cheer filled the air, James Maxwell cleared his throat and stepped to the microphone.

SELECTING DETAILS FROM THE STORY. Each of the following sentences helps you understand the story. Complete each sentence below by putting an *x* in the box next to the correct answer.

1. James Maxwell often wondered what would have happened if he had
   - ☐ a. become a doctor or a teacher.
   - ☐ b. decided to be a scientist.
   - ☐ c. followed the path that Gerald Adams took.

2. As Maxwell stared at the shiny metal spaceship, he
   - ☐ a. was glad he was not aboard that rocket.
   - ☐ b. wished he were aboard that rocket.
   - ☐ c. decided to train to become an astronaut.

3. The Director of Space Exploration walked across the platform and
   - ☐ a. cut the ribbon in front of the spaceship.
   - ☐ b. congratulated each astronaut.
   - ☐ c. shook hands with James Maxwell.

4. At the end of the story we learn that Maxwell is
   - ☐ a. one of the astronauts.
   - ☐ b. a famous lawyer.
   - ☐ c. President of the World Republic.

HANDLING STORY ELEMENTS. Each of the following questions reviews your understanding of story elements. Put an *x* in the box next to the correct answer to each question.

1. What happened last in the *plot* of "The Cog"?
   - ☐ a. The crew of the *President* came onto the speaker's stand.
   - ☐ b. James Maxwell stepped to the microphone.
   - ☐ c. A speaker told the crowd about the glorious conquest of space.

2. Who is the *main character* in the story?
   - ☐ a. Gerald Adams
   - ☐ b. James Maxwell
   - ☐ c. the Director of Space Exploration

3. Which sentence best *characterizes* James Maxwell?
   - ☐ a. He longed to be an astronaut.
   - ☐ b. He longed to return to law school.
   - ☐ c. He wished that he had gained fame and fortune.

4. When is "The Cog" *set*?
   - ☐ a. in the future
   - ☐ b. in the past
   - ☐ c. at the present time

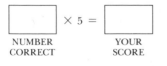

☐ × 5 = ☐

NUMBER CORRECT YOUR SCORE

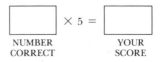

☐ × 5 = ☐

NUMBER CORRECT YOUR SCORE

OBSERVING NEW VOCABULARY WORDS. Answer the following vocabulary questions by putting an *x* in the box next to the correct answer. The vocabulary words are printed in **boldface** in the story. If you wish, look back at the words before you answer the questions.

1. The rocket had broken apart, bursting into a million fragments. The word *fragments* means
   □ a. broken pieces.
   □ b. shining stars.
   □ c. beautiful pictures.

2. He thought he would probably die in bed, an old man too feeble to make it to the next room. The word *feeble* means
   □ a. worried.
   □ b. annoyed.
   □ c. weak.

3. Many spectators had come to see the launching of the spaceship. *Spectators* are people who
   □ a. are paid to play sports.
   □ b. look on without taking part.
   □ c. build rockets.

4. Maxwell went to law school because his family was very practical and suggested that he do the sensible thing. What is the meaning of the word *sensible*?
   □ a. reasonable; wise
   □ b. enjoyable; pleasant
   □ c. unusual; strange

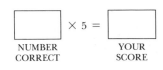

NUMBER CORRECT   × 5 =   YOUR SCORE

COMPLETING A CLOZE PASSAGE. Complete the following paragraph by filling in each blank with one of the words listed in the box below. Each of the words appears in the story. Since there are five words and four blanks, one word in the group will not be used.

Without a telescope, you can see only about 2,000 of the _____ of
stars in the universe. Of course during the day, it is easy to see the star that is closest to Earth—the _____ .
Compared to other _____ ,
the sun is not large. But since it is "only" 93,000,000 miles away, it appears bigger and _____ than any other star.

---

millions   sun

machinery

stars   brighter

NUMBER CORRECT   × 5 =   YOUR SCORE

52

KNOWING HOW TO READ CRITICALLY. Each of the following questions will help you to think critically about the selection. Put an *x* in the box next to the correct answer.

1. The story suggests that if Maxwell could live his life over, he
   - ☐ a. wouldn't change a thing.
   - ☐ b. would be an astronaut.
   - ☐ c. would take a practical job in the community.

2. Which statement is true?
   - ☐ a. Very few people came to see the spacecraft take off.
   - ☐ b. Maxwell's family encouraged him to become an astronaut.
   - ☐ c. Although Maxwell was President of the World Republic, he still considered himself a cog in the machine.

3. Maxwell respected Gerald Adams because Gerald had
   - ☐ a. been a friend.
   - ☐ b. gone to school with him.
   - ☐ c. followed his dream.

4. During the ceremonies, Maxwell must have been
   - ☐ a. inside the rocket.
   - ☐ b. on the lawn.
   - ☐ c. on the speaker's platform.

Questions for Writing and Discussion

- According to an old saying: "The grass is always greener on the other side of the fence." How might this saying be applied to "The Cog"?
- Why do you think the author called the spaceship the *President*? What does this suggest about James Maxwell?
- At the end of the story, James Maxwell "cleared his throat and stepped to the microphone." Think about what had been going through Maxwell's mind. Then tell what you think he might have said to the crowd.

Use the boxes below to total your scores for the exercises. Then write your score on pages 150 and 151.

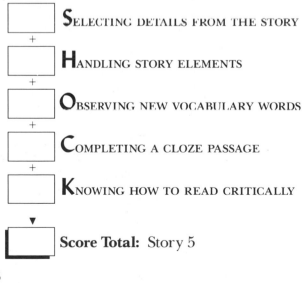

	SELECTING DETAILS FROM THE STORY
+	
	HANDLING STORY ELEMENTS
+	
	OBSERVING NEW VOCABULARY WORDS
+	
	COMPLETING A CLOZE PASSAGE
+	
	KNOWING HOW TO READ CRITICALLY
▼	
	Score Total: Story 5

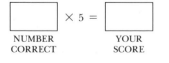

× 5 =

NUMBER   YOUR
CORRECT   SCORE

53

6

The Scholarship

by Minfong Ho

*N*ow listen," the teacher said in a deep solemn voice. "We don't have much time left, and I have an important announcement to make. You all know that I received the results of the government examination early this morning. The best student among you will get free schooling away in the big city school."

An excited murmur swelled up from the class. The scholarship! He was talking about the scholarship at last! Dawan stole a quick glance at her brother, but he was staring at the teacher, his whole body filled with suspense.

"Getting the scholarship isn't just winning a prize," the teacher continued sternly. "It also means the student will be bearing heavy responsibilities. What kind of attitude should that student have toward continuing school?"

Kwai raised his hand hesitantly. "He should learn what is useful to his people, and come back to help the village after he has finished learning."

"But how will the student know what will be useful and what will not?" the teacher challenged. "First, that student must learn how to think, to grasp what is wrong with the society, to understand the rules which create these injustices, and . . ." He stopped suddenly and demanded, "And what?"

"And change it for fairer rules," Dawan whispered softly.

The teacher caught her soft answer. "Yes, and change it for a fairer system," he repeated in a low, solemn voice.

Then, peering down at her, he asked, "Well, Dawan, do you think you could do all that?"

"Me?" Dawan asked faintly. Behind her a classmate **snickered** loudly, and there was a general round of giggling in the small classroom.

"Well, child?" the teacher continued. His tone was stern but still kind.

Dawan looked up at him in confusion. Why was he deliberately picking on her like this? She glanced around her quickly, and felt as if she was swimming in a sea of wide, teasing eyes.

"Please, sir, never mind me," Dawan said. "Just tell us who won the scholarship."

There was a long pause. Distant sounds of a dog barking, of villagers singing in the rice fields, of the rustling of palms floated in the open windows. Streaks of sunlight darted between the desk and chair legs, forming patterns of light and shadow.

"But, child," the teacher finally said, his voice sounding far away, "you did."

After the last bell rang, Dawan was surrounded by a crowd of curious and chattering classmates. They fired so many questions at her that Dawan, shy and reserved as she was, felt panicky. Gripping the edge of her wooden desk, she looked around desperately for Kwai.

But her brother was not among the crowd. She searched the whole room with quick, frightened eyes until she saw him. He was standing alone in the doorway, clutching his pile of schoolbooks and his loneliness, silently watching her in the midst of her admirers.

She called out to him, but he only turned away and stalked out abruptly.

With a knotted feeling in her stomach, Dawan forced her way through the crowd after her brother. But in the schoolyard she was again surrounded, this time by the monks that lived in the small temple around the corner.

As she elbowed her way through them as politely as she could, someone called cheerfully after her, "Don't forget to tell your whole family the good news!"

That cheerful voice seemed to ring in her ears now, as her bare feet trailed along the path, toward home. "Kwai already knows 'the good news,' " she thought to herself uneasily, "and he hates me for it."

As she approached the house, she heard the familiar sounds of her mother singing to the baby, and of chickens clucking as they pecked the dirt underneath the stilts of the house. Her grandmother was sitting on a tree stump, tired and dignified looking, sprinkling feed for the chickens and watching Dawan's father repair the chicken coop.

"Has Kwai come home yet, Grandmama?" Dawan asked, carefully putting her schoolbooks on a low workbench.

The old woman was about to answer when Dawan's mother walked out onto the veranda above them. She called down to her daughter, "That brother of yours! I don't know what he's up to now! He was here just a few minutes ago, but rushed away again. And he promised me he'd cut me some bamboo shoots for dinner tonight, too! Dawan, will you help me to . . ."

But Dawan was not listening anymore. She gazed toward the fields, then dropped her eyes with a soft sigh.

"Child, is there anything wrong?" her old grandmother asked sharply. She had a way of sensing things, this old woman, and when she spoke like that people usually listened and waited.

Dawan pulled at her earlobes, scratched her knee, shifted her weight from one foot to the other, refusing all the while to look at anybody.

Her father became impatient first and grunted, "Well, Dawan, what is it?"

Dawan glanced over at him and suddenly noticed that the big pile of rice sacks was gone. So the landlord's man had taken everything away already. Her heart sank. Her father would be in an even worse mood than usual, making her news that much harder to break. She tried to speak, but the fear in her heart held back her words.

There were only the sounds of the lazy afternoon breeze and of the chickens clucking thoughtfully to themselves. Dawan's eyes flickered over her mother, at her stern father, and her quiet grandmother. But they finally focused on a shiny puddle by the big brown rain barrel.

Staring at the puddle, she finally spoke, "You know that prize that the government gives out after the big examination?" Even without looking up she could sense her father grow tense. This meant so much to him, too. "Well, the best student," she glanced quickly at her father's unsmiling face and stumbled on, "or, or at least the one who happens to get the best marks, well, wins the prize and gets to go to the city and continue to . . ."

"I know all that!" Dawan's father snapped. "What about it?"

In the pause that followed, a tiny green frog hopped out of the puddle onto the dust, its bright eyes blinking at Dawan. The little frog looked so determined and eager that Dawan found strength in it and continued haltingly, "I won the prize. I can go to the city and study more now." She stole another glance at her father. "Can't I?"

The frog hopped away from the puddle, then stood very still, blinking at the vast world about him. Dawan addressed the puddle again. "Please, can I? . . ."

"And Kwai? What about Kwai? He won nothing?" Her father's voice was rough and tinged with a hard wonder. Dawan sensed the pain in her father, and did not dare to look directly into his eyes.

"There is only one prize," she whispered.

Dawan looked timidly at her father and this time their eyes met. There was a long pause, then he said angrily, "You took your own brother's chance away from him!" He flung down the hammer he had been holding, and stalked away to the rice fields.

The grandmother, mother, and daughter all watched him stride away. Dawan kept quiet, for she was afraid of angering her elders. For a while no one stirred. Then the grandmother slowly straightened up from the tree stump, and walked with slow careful steps over to Dawan.

"Child," she said, touching her granddaughter's hand lightly, "I'm proud of you."

"You should not encourage her so!" Dawan's mother called from the veranda. "You know her father won't let her go. She'll be even more disappointed if you praise her now. At least spare her that."

Dawan felt her heart sinking. How was it her mother could be so loving and full of laughter one moment, and so biting and sour the next—and sometimes, like now, even both at once?

The grandmother looked directly at her own daughter. In a voice quiet with **conviction**, she stated, "I do what I think is right."

They continued to glare at each other. Suddenly the baby whimpered, and the mother had to shift her attention to it. The grandmother gave a short grunt of satisfaction, and walked slowly back to the shade beneath the house.

Dawan picked up her schoolbooks. Her grandmother suddenly called her over.

"Child, never mind those books for now. We're going to Noi's house," she ordered.

"Wait, what are you trying to do?" Dawan's mother asked sharply. "Why do you want to take Dawan to Noi's house?"

The old woman answered calmly, "Noi and her husband have both lived in the city before. They know its ways better than any of us, and can tell us what it is like for a young girl to go to school there. Besides," she added innocently, "they like Dawan a lot."

"I see what you're up to!" Dawan's mother shouted to the grandmother. "You're going to try and talk Noi into arguing for Dawan in front of her father, aren't you? You think that Noi will trot on over and, just like that, convince my husband to let Dawan go off to the city school? There's no hope in that! He'll never think it right for Kwai's sister to go in his place."

"Mother, would *you* let me go?" Dawan asked. Her mother did not answer. Dawan repeated her question. "You would let me go, wouldn't you?"

Still there was only a stubborn silence.

Finally her mother sighed heavily and muttered, "It is not my place to say anything." She turned her gaze away, avoiding Dawan's eyes.

"That," replied the grandmother, "is what you happen to think! And that is why Dawan and I will have to walk three kilometers to Noi's home to ask her to speak in your place." She beckoned to Dawan and said crisply, "Come, child, let us go."

Dawan looked helplessly at the notebooks still in her hands. Then she walked over to her mother, and standing on tiptoe, stretched her arm upward to hand the books to her mother on the veranda. Her mother automatically reached down for them.

"Mother, I am going now," Dawan said, her voice small but determined. To her surprise there was no scolding or protest. So Dawan turned and joined her grandmother.

The old woman had already started off on her own—a bent figure **hobbling** step by step along the narrow dirt path toward Noi's house. Dawan **sprinted** the short distance to catch up with her grandmother.

They had taken less than twenty steps when they heard someone calling. Turning around, they saw Dawan's mother running after them in short, quick steps.

"Wait!" she called.

They paused until Dawan's mother caught up with them. Standing close together in a little triangle, the three of them looked warily at each other.

The grandmother finally broke the silence. "Three kilometers is a long way," she murmured.

"Especially under this hot sun," Dawan's mother added quickly.

"And I am getting old," said the grandmother.

Then Dawan's mother said, "I will walk the three kilometers with Dawan for you."

"It is kind of you to do that," said the grandmother, "for the way is long and hot."

Then turning away, she began to walk slowly back home.

SELECTING DETAILS FROM THE STORY.
Each of the following sentences helps
you understand the story. Complete each
sentence below by putting an *x* in the
box next to the correct answer.

1. The teacher stated that the student
   who won the scholarship would
   ☐ a. receive a large cash prize.
   ☐ b. be given an excellent job.
   ☐ c. get free schooling in the big
      city school.

2. Dawan's father thought that the
   scholarship should go to
   ☐ a. Dawan.
   ☐ b. Kwai.
   ☐ c. one of Noi's children.

3. When Dawan's grandmother
   learned that Dawan had won the
   scholarship, she
   ☐ a. was proud of Dawan and
      encouraged her.
   ☐ b. felt very sorry for Dawan.
   ☐ c. thought that Dawan would be
      wise to refuse it.

4. At the end of the story, Dawan's mother
   decided to
   ☐ a. punish Dawan.
   ☐ b. stay home with the baby.
   ☐ c. walk with Dawan to Noi's house.

HANDLING STORY ELEMENTS. Each of
the following questions reviews your
understanding of story elements. Put
an *x* in the box next to the correct
answer to each question.

1. "The Scholarship" is *set* in a
   ☐ a. large city in the United States.
   ☐ b. village in Asia.
   ☐ c. thriving factory town.

2. What happened first in the *plot* of
   the story?
   ☐ a. Dawan and her grandmother
      started off to Noi's house.
   ☐ b. The teacher announced who won
      the scholarship.
   ☐ c. Dawan's father flung down his
      hammer and stalked away.

3. "You took your own brother's chance
   away from him!" This line of *dialogue*
   was spoken by Dawan's
   ☐ a. father.
   ☐ b. mother.
   ☐ c. grandmother.

4. What is the *mood* of "The
   Scholarship"?
   ☐ a. humorous
   ☐ b. mysterious
   ☐ c. serious

NUMBER
CORRECT

× 5 =

YOUR
SCORE

NUMBER
CORRECT

× 5 =

YOUR
SCORE

OBSERVING NEW VOCABULARY WORDS.
Answer the following vocabulary questions by putting an *x* in the box next to the correct answer. The vocabulary words are printed in **boldface** in the story. If you wish, look back at the words before you answer the questions.

1. A classmate snickered loudly at Dawan, and there was giggling in the classroom. The word *snickered* means
   □ a. laughed.
   □ b. praised.
   □ c. fought.

2. The old woman started off—a bent figure hobbling step by step along the narrow dirt path. What is the meaning of the word *hobbling*?
   □ a. dashing madly
   □ b. skipping briskly
   □ c. walking awkwardly

3. Dawan sprinted the short distance to catch up with her grandmother. The word *sprinted* means
   □ a. shouted loudly.
   □ b. ran at full speed.
   □ c. measured carefully.

4. "I do what I think is right," the grandmother said with conviction. As used here, the word *conviction* means a
   □ a. feeling of doubt.
   □ b. strong belief in something.
   □ c. sense of amazement.

COMPLETING A CLOZE PASSAGE. Complete the following paragraph by filling in each blank with one of the words listed in the box below. Each of the words appears in the story. Since there are five words and four blanks, one word in the group will not be used.

If you enjoyed "The Scholarship," we _____ you to read *Sing to the Dawn* by Minfong Ho. The story takes place in a _____ in southeast Asia. Among the characters are Dawan and her parents and _____.

If this seems _____, that is not surprising. "The Scholarship" is taken from the novel, *Sing to the Dawn*.

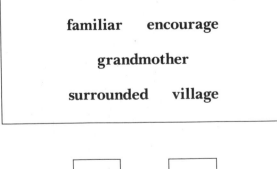

familiar   encourage

grandmother

surrounded   village

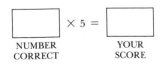

NUMBER
CORRECT

YOUR
SCORE

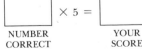

NUMBER
CORRECT

YOUR
SCORE

KNOWING HOW TO READ CRITICALLY. Each of the following questions will help you to think critically about the selection. Put an *x* in the box next to the correct answer.

1. When Dawan heard that she had won the scholarship, she probably felt
   ☐ a. angry.
   ☐ b. surprised.
   ☐ c. upset.

2. Kwai's actions after his sister won the scholarship showed that he
   ☐ a. was proud of her.
   ☐ b. was hurt and disappointed.
   ☐ c. expected her to win it all along.

3. We may infer (figure out) that Dawan's family was
   ☐ a. poor.
   ☐ b. wealthy.
   ☐ c. extremely well educated.

4. The character who changed most during the course of the story was Kwai's
   ☐ a. mother.
   ☐ b. father.
   ☐ c. grandmother.

Questions for Writing and Discussion

• When Dawan won the scholarship, her father was not pleased. Why? Suppose you were a friend of the family. What might you say to him to change his point of view?

• In some ways, Dawan's grandmother was more modern than her own daughter. Do you agree with that statement? Explain.

• What, do you think, is likely to happen as a result of the meeting at Noi's house? Give reasons for your answer.

Use the boxes below to total your scores for the exercises. Then write your score on pages 150 and 151.

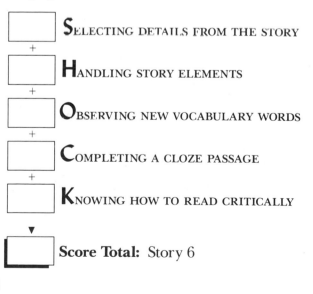

☐ **S**ELECTING DETAILS FROM THE STORY

+

☐ **H**ANDLING STORY ELEMENTS

+

☐ **O**BSERVING NEW VOCABULARY WORDS

+

☐ **C**OMPLETING A CLOZE PASSAGE

+

☐ **K**NOWING HOW TO READ CRITICALLY

▼

☐ **Score Total:** Story 6

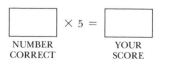

☐ × 5 = ☐

NUMBER   YOUR
CORRECT   SCORE

7

The Invaders

by Jack Ritchie

*N*one of them left the ship on the first day of its arrival, but I knew they would be watching carefully for signs of human life.

The skies were dark with swiftly moving clouds, and the cold wind moved high in the trees. Thin snow drifted slowly to the ground.

From the cover of the forest, I now watched as a small, heavily armed group of them left the large craft. When they reached the edge of the woods, they hesitated for a few moments. Then they moved cautiously forward.

I had seen them before and I knew that in appearance, at least, they were not monsters. They looked very much like us. There were some differences, of course, but all in all, we were really quite similar to them.

I met them first when I was almost a boy and I had been without **caution**. I approached them and they seemed friendly. But then suddenly they seized me and carried me off in their strange ship.

It was a long journey to their land, and when our ship made a landing, I was shown about and exhibited.

I saw their cities, and I was shown plants and animals completely strange to me. I learned to wear their clothing and even to eat their food.

They taught me to communicate in their strange and difficult tongue until I could, at times, even think in their language.

I had almost given up the hope of ever seeing my home again. But one day they put me back on one of their ships and told me that they were returning me because they wished to establish friendly relations with my people. But by now, I knew enough of them to know that this was not true. However, I nodded and smiled and watched for my opportunity to escape.

When the ship landed, I went out with the first search party. It was near evening, and as the darkness gathered, I edged away from them. Finally I fled into the blackness and safety of the forest.

They came after me, of course, but I was hidden deep in the woods where they could not find me.

Finally they gave up and I watched their ship become smaller and finally disappear, and I hoped earnestly that they would never return.

But now they were back again.

I felt a coldness inside of me as I watched them moving slowly through the trees. They seemed somehow different from the others who had been here before. It was not so much in their appearance as in their manner— the way they walked, the way they looked about with questioning and **speculating** eyes.

Slowly, I realized that this time they were not here on just another raid for a captive or two.

This time they had come to stay.

What could we do now? Could we **lure** them deeper into the forest and kill them? Could we take their weapons and learn how to use them?

No, I thought with **despair**. There were so many more of the invaders on the ship. And more weapons. They would come out and hunt us down like animals. They would hunt us down and kill us all.

I sighed. We must find out what it was that they wanted this time and whatever it might be, we must learn to adjust and to hope for the best.

But I still retreated silently before them, afraid to approach. I watched them search the ground ahead of them and knew they were looking for footprints, for some signs of life. But there was not yet enough snow on the ground to track us down.

Their strangely colored eyes glanced about suspiciously, warily. They were cautious, yes.

They could be cruel, I knew. I had seen with my own eyes how they treated their animals and even their own kind.

I sighed again. Yes, we could be cruel, too. In this respect we could not claim to be superior to the invaders.

They paused now in a clearing, their eyes gleaming beneath their helmets.

It was time for me to approach them.

I took a deep breath and stepped into the open.

Their weapons quickly pointed at me.

"Welcome," I said.

They stared at me, and then one of them turned to their bearded leader. "It appears that he can speak some English, Captain Standish.[1] "

"Welcome," I said again. But I wondered what they would do to my land and my people now.

---

1. Captain Standish: Miles Standish (1584?–1656) was an English colonist who came to America with the Pilgrims on the *Mayflower* and helped establish Plymouth Colony in America.

SELECTING DETAILS FROM THE STORY. Each of the following sentences helps you understand the story. Complete each sentence below by putting an *x* in the box next to the correct answer.

1. When the narrator (the person who tells the story) first met the strangers, they
   - ☐ a. welcomed him warmly.
   - ☐ b. seized him and carried him off.
   - ☐ c. scared him away.

2. When the narrator returned to his land with the strangers, he
   - ☐ a. edged away from them and escaped into the forest.
   - ☐ b. introduced the strangers to his people.
   - ☐ c. helped the strangers adjust to the new land.

3. The narrator realized that it would be useless to fight the strangers because
   - ☐ a. there were many more of them on the ship.
   - ☐ b. they had many powerful weapons.
   - ☐ c. of both of the above.

4. At the end of the story, the narrator was concerned about
   - ☐ a. whether the strangers would remember him.
   - ☐ b. whether the strangers would be able to understand him.
   - ☐ c. what the strangers would do to his land and his people.

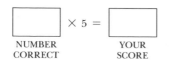

NUMBER CORRECT × 5 = YOUR SCORE

HANDLING STORY ELEMENTS. Each of the following questions reviews your understanding of story elements. Put an *x* in the box next to the correct answer to each question.

1. What happened last in the *plot* of "The Invaders"?
   - ☐ a. The narrator learned to wear the strangers' clothing and to eat their food.
   - ☐ b. The strangers searched for the narrator without success.
   - ☐ c. One of the strangers said, "It appears that he can speak some English."

2. Which sentence best *characterizes* the narrator?
   - ☐ a. He was worried about what the return of the strangers would mean.
   - ☐ b. He was certain that the strangers would be friendly.
   - ☐ c. He knew that the strangers would never act cruelly.

3. In this story, there is *conflict* between the
   - ☐ a. narrator and his people.
   - ☐ b. narrator and the strangers.
   - ☐ c. strangers and their leader, Captain Standish.

4. Where is "The Invaders" *set*?
   - ☐ a. on a distant planet
   - ☐ b. in England
   - ☐ c. in America

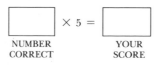

NUMBER CORRECT × 5 = YOUR SCORE

OBSERVING NEW VOCABULARY WORDS. Answer the following vocabulary questions by putting an *x* in the box next to the correct answer. The vocabulary words are printed in **boldface** in the story. If you wish, look back at the words before you answer the questions.

1. He thought, with despair, that there were too many of them to fight. What is the meaning of the word *despair*?
   ☐ a. eagerness
   ☐ b. enjoyment
   ☐ c. loss of hope

2. As a boy he had been without caution and had approached the strangers. Which of the following best defines (gives the meaning of) the word *caution*?
   ☐ a. care or concern with safety
   ☐ b. curiosity or a desire to know
   ☐ c. power or strength

3. He wondered if they could lure the invaders deeper into the forest and then kill them. The word *lure* means
   ☐ a. push away.
   ☐ b. draw into.
   ☐ c. insult.

4. The strangers walked slowly as they looked around with questioning and speculating eyes. As used here, the word *speculating* means
   ☐ a. wondering about or guessing.
   ☐ b. dull or dim.
   ☐ c. buying in order to make a profit.

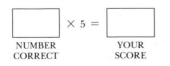

NUMBER CORRECT   × 5 =   YOUR SCORE

COMPLETING A CLOZE PASSAGE. Complete the following paragraph by filling in each blank with one of the words listed in the box below. Each of the words appears in the story. Since there are five words and four blanks, one word in the group will not be used.

In 1620, _____ colonists
                          1

crossed the Atlantic on a ship named the

Mayflower. After a difficult and dangerous

_____ , they arrived in America
          2

and settled at Plymouth. There they

_____ Plymouth Colony. It is
          3

interesting to note that the colonists left

Plymouth, England, and named their new

_____ Plymouth, Massachusetts.
          4

silently	English
established	
colony	journey

NUMBER CORRECT   × 5 =   YOUR SCORE

68

KNOWING HOW TO READ CRITICALLY. Each of the following questions will help you to think critically about the selection. Put an *x* in the box next to the correct answer.

1. Which statement is true?
   - ☐ a. The strangers came to the new land on a spaceship.
   - ☐ b. The author tries to make you think that the strangers are aliens, or creatures from another planet.
   - ☐ c. The author was glad to see the strangers return.

2. The story probably takes place during the winter because
   - ☐ a. the narrator felt cold when he observed the strangers.
   - ☐ b. the strangers were wearing very warm clothing.
   - ☐ c. the strangers looked for footprints, but there was not enough snow on the ground.

3. Who were the strangers?
   - ☐ a. aliens from a distant planet
   - ☐ b. Native Americans
   - ☐ c. English colonists

4. Who was the narrator?
   - ☐ a. a Native American
   - ☐ b. a visitor from space
   - ☐ c. an English colonist

Questions for Writing and Discussion
- Why do you think the author called the story "The Invaders"? Is this a good title for the story? Explain.
- The narrator was a very brave and intelligent person. Present evidence from the story to support that statement.
- In "The Invaders," events are seen through the eyes of the narrator and are told in his words. Do you think that makes the story more powerful? Explain your answer.

Use the boxes below to total your scores for the exercises. Then write your score on pages 150 and 151.

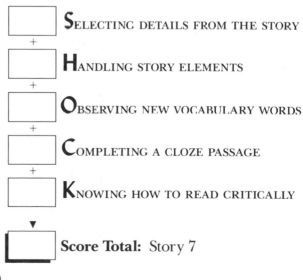

SELECTING DETAILS FROM THE STORY
+
HANDLING STORY ELEMENTS
+
OBSERVING NEW VOCABULARY WORDS
+
COMPLETING A CLOZE PASSAGE
+
KNOWING HOW TO READ CRITICALLY
▼
Score Total: Story 7

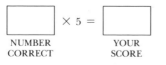

× 5 =

NUMBER   YOUR
CORRECT   SCORE

8

Blue Eyes Far Away

by MacKinlay Kantor

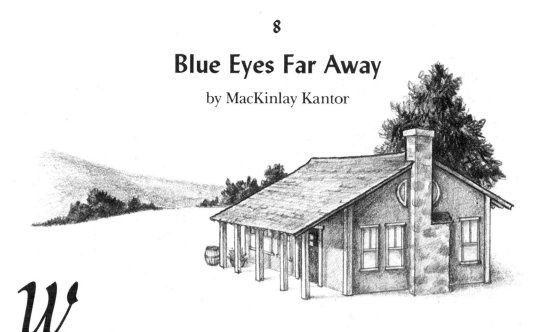

*W*hen neighbors climbed the steep hill road to bring Esther Lee the news they did not want to bring, they found their task easier than they had expected.

She was sitting on a bench under the old cedar tree. Her blue eyes seemed very empty and blank behind her glasses.

"Mrs. Lee," said George Dutton uneasily, "we came to tell you—there's been an accident and your husband was—. They took him to the hospital. I think you'd better come, right away."

Joseph Lee's wife didn't say anything. Slowly she rose to her feet. The wide black purse on her lap slid to the ground.

George Dutton turned away while his wife put her arm around Esther Lee's shoulders. "Now, Mrs. Lee—he's hurt bad, but maybe he'll be all right."

"It was an automobile accident," the farmer said. "The highway police have got the fellow that hit him, too. If it's possible to convict him, we're going to do it."

Convict him, thought Esther Lee. That meant, then, that Joseph was—

"Can we go now?" she asked.

"Yes. Our car's right out here at the gate. Don't you want to lock your house? And what about your purse?"

"Leave them be," the woman said quietly.

It was a **flimsy** case, a weak case at best. It was really no case at all—except that a man had been killed when his car was struck by the powerful, bright red automobile of a young man.

The curve in the road had been deserted at the time of the accident. The two men were the only ones there. But noise of the crash had drawn people from all directions.

The police checked the record of Archie Stolt, the man who drove the red automobile. It was found that he had been involved in several other accidents. His reputation for wild and **reckless** driving was known. But you can't convict a man on his reputation, said the young fellow's lawyers.

The young man was charged with manslaughter. But after that things moved slowly.

Interest in the case was not great. Joseph Lee was neither a wealthy nor a well-known man. The courtroom was not crowded. The defense knew that in the case of the *State of New Jersey* versus *Archie Stolt,* matters would be simple, routine. The case would cost Archie Stolt money. But he could well afford it. The defense did not know, however, that the night before the trial began, a small, elderly woman in a shabby cloth dress and old black hat went to see the **prosecutor**.

The defense lawyers for Mr. Stolt shrugged when they saw her sitting in court. A weak attempt, they whispered, to get sympathy from the jury.

Esther Lee was the last witness called by the State. Earlier they had tried to put in the record Archie Stolt's other accidents and his bad reputation. But these were not allowed. Mr. Stolt watched comfortably, unworried, as the frail woman said she was Esther Lee, widow of Joseph Lee who had been killed.

"Where do you live, Mrs. Lee?" came the prosecutor's question.

"On Watchung Mountain."

"Were you home on the afternoon of June 20th, at about 5:30 P.M.?"

"Yes, sir," said Esther Lee.

The lawyer cleared his throat. "Mrs. Lee, how long have you lived there?"

"Well," she said in her mild voice, "quite a while. See, when Joseph and I were first married, we lived down at Barnegat. He fished. We lived there for thirty-one years. And then his nephew left him this place up on Watchung Mountain. We were getting older, so we moved up there. We lived there for nearly eleven years. We—"

"Your Honor," said Archie Stolt's lawyer, "I object. The answers by the witness have nothing to do with the case and are beside the point. They are only intended to gain sympathy for—"

The judge rapped. "Objection sustained."

The next question came like an explosion through the close air of the courtroom. "Mrs. Lee, did you see the accident in which your husband met his death?"

The woman nodded yes. Her reply was lost in the sudden stir and scuffling as people moved forward.

"Tell the court what you saw."

"Well," said Esther Lee, "Joseph had gone to Union. He drove there every day because he had good customers there. I sat out in front, always, to watch for him. I always used to do that, when he fished at Barnegat—"

Archie Stolt's lawyer was on his feet, but the prosecutor motioned him into his chair. "Tell only about the accident, please," he said to Esther Lee.

Esther Lee's blue eyes were wet. "I watched Joseph's old car come around a bend in the road," she said slowly, "and he was on the right side of the road. And then the red car came from the other way—on the wrong side of the road. And—Joseph's car swung out toward the middle—to try and miss it, I guess. But the other car swung out, too. . . . They hit. That's all, sir. But the red car was on the wrong side of—"

73

"Your Honor!" cried the lawyer for the defense.

Archie Stolt settled back into his chair with a scornful smile on his face. They couldn't pull anything like that and get away with it.

"I object!" said the lawyer for the defense. "It was not possible for Esther Lee to have seen the accident from so far away! Not possible! The scene of the accident is miles from her home. I—"

The judge turned and looked solemnly at the old woman. "I must remind you," he said, "that telling a lie here is a very serious **offense**. You have sworn to tell nothing but the truth. How far is it from your home to the scene of the accident?"

"Must be a good three miles," whispered Esther Lee.

Three miles. . . . People in the courtroom shook their heads.

The woman's rough fingers fumbled as she opened the black purse on her lap. "I always watched for Joseph, though," she said. "Just like I used to do when he'd come in with his fish at Barnegat."

She held up a shiny brass telescope. "This was his," she explained. "I always watched for Joseph, when he came home."

SELECTING DETAILS FROM THE STORY.
Each of the following sentences helps
you understand the story. Complete each
sentence below by putting an *x* in the
box next to the correct answer.

1. The neighbors told Esther Lee that
   - ☐ a. she had to appear in court.
   - ☐ b. the police wanted to speak to her.
   - ☐ c. her husband had been badly hurt.

2. The police learned that Archie Stolt
   - ☐ a. had been in several other accidents.
   - ☐ b. had never been in an accident before.
   - ☐ c. could not afford a lawyer.

3. When Archie Stolt's lawyers saw Mrs. Lee sitting in court, they
   - ☐ a. shrugged and were not worried.
   - ☐ b. were very concerned about what she might say.
   - ☐ c. asked the judge to prevent her from giving evidence.

4. Esther Lee witnessed the accident because she
   - ☐ a. was in the automobile at the time of the accident.
   - ☐ b. was standing on the road when the accident took place.
   - ☐ c. saw the accident through a telescope.

HANDLING STORY ELEMENTS. Each of
the following questions reviews your
understanding of story elements. Put
an *x* in the box next to the correct
answer to each question.

1. What happened first in the *plot* of the story?
   - ☐ a. Esther Lee described how the accident took place.
   - ☐ b. The neighbors brought Mrs. Lee the bad news.
   - ☐ c. The police checked the record of Archie Stolt.

2. Which pair of words best *characterizes* Esther Lee?
   - ☐ a. young; wealthy
   - ☐ b. small; elderly
   - ☐ c. tall; rugged

3. The ending of "Blue Eyes Far Away" is *set*
   - ☐ a. in a courtroom.
   - ☐ b. in a police station.
   - ☐ c. on a deserted country road.

4. Which sentence best describes the *theme* of the story?
   - ☐ a. A man is killed when he is struck by a powerful, bright red automobile.
   - ☐ b. It is not possible to convict a man on his poor reputation.
   - ☐ c. The widow of a man killed in an accident proves to be a witness to the event.

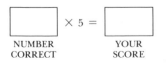

× 5 =

NUMBER
CORRECT

YOUR
SCORE

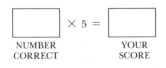

× 5 =

NUMBER
CORRECT

YOUR
SCORE

OBSERVING NEW VOCABULARY WORDS. Answer the following vocabulary questions by putting an *x* in the box next to the correct answer. The vocabulary words are printed in **boldface** in the story. If you wish, look back at the words before you answer the questions.

1. It was a flimsy case, a weak case at best. What is the meaning of the word *flimsy*?
   □ a. strong
   □ b. delightful
   □ c. shaky

2. The judge reminded Mrs. Lee that telling a lie in court is a very serious offense. As used here, the word *offense* means
   □ a. idea.
   □ b. crime.
   □ c. joke.

3. Archie Stolt had a reputation for wild and reckless driving. The word *reckless* means
   □ a. slow or unhurried.
   □ b. careful or thoughtful.
   □ c. careless or risky.

4. The night before the trial began, Mrs. Lee went to see the prosecutor. A *prosecutor* is a person who
   □ a. accuses, or brings charges against, another person.
   □ b. is a witness at an accident.
   □ c. is one of the members of a jury.

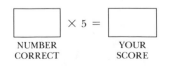

NUMBER CORRECT × 5 = YOUR SCORE

COMPLETING A CLOZE PASSAGE. Complete the following paragraph by filling in each blank with one of the words listed in the box below. Each of the words appears in the story. Since there are five words and four blanks, one word in the group will not be used.

Most people _____ that it

is unsafe to drink and drive. But here

are some other _____ tips

all drivers should follow. Don't

_____ if you are ill—or if

you are taking medicine that makes you

feel sleepy. On long trips, plan to rest every

few hours. You are more likely to have a(n)

_____ when you are tired.

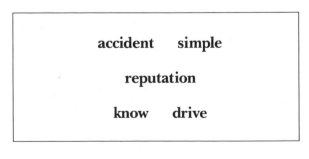

accident   simple

reputation

know   drive

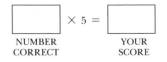

NUMBER CORRECT × 5 = YOUR SCORE

76

KNOWING HOW TO READ CRITICALLY. Each of the following questions will help you to think critically about the selection. Put an *x* in the box next to the correct answer.

1. Which statement is true?
   - ☐ a. Joseph Lee had been driving on the wrong side of the road.
   - ☐ b. Archie Stolt had been driving on the wrong side of the road.
   - ☐ c. Both men had been driving on the wrong side of the road.

2. When Archie Stolt entered the courtroom, he
   - ☐ a. did not appear worried.
   - ☐ b. was afraid that he was going to be convicted of the crime.
   - ☐ c. was wondering if he should confess.

3. At first, it appeared that Archie Stolt would be found innocent because
   - ☐ a. he had done nothing wrong.
   - ☐ b. no one, apparently, had seen the accident.
   - ☐ c. he could prove that he was an excellent driver.

4. When the neighbors told Mrs. Lee the bad news, they found their task easier than they had expected. Why?
   - ☐ a. She didn't really care about her husband.
   - ☐ b. She didn't fully understand what they were telling her.
   - ☐ c. She had already seen the accident through the telescope.

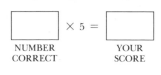

NUMBER CORRECT   ×5 =   YOUR SCORE

Questions for Writing and Discussion
- The judge warned Esther Lee about telling a lie in court. Why did it appear, at first, that Mrs. Lee was lying? What reason might she have had for telling a lie?
- Mrs. Lee loved her husband very much. Find evidence from the story to support that statement.
- What, do you think, will happen as a result of what Mrs. Lee told the jury? Give reasons for your answer.

Use the boxes below to total your scores for the exercises. Then write your score on pages 150 and 151.

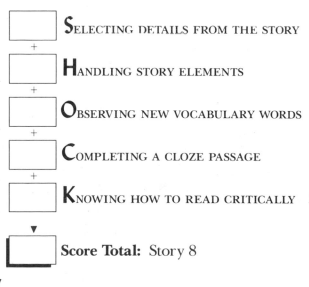

SELECTING DETAILS FROM THE STORY

HANDLING STORY ELEMENTS

OBSERVING NEW VOCABULARY WORDS

COMPLETING A CLOZE PASSAGE

KNOWING HOW TO READ CRITICALLY

Score Total: Story 8

9

The Cow-Tail Switch

FOLKTALE FROM LIBERIA

*N*ear the edge of the Liberian rain forest was the village of Kundi. Its rice fields spread in all directions. Cattle grazed in the grassland near the river. Smoke from the fires in the round clay houses seeped through the palmleaf roofs, and from a distance these faint columns of smoke seemed to hover over the village. Men and boys fished in the river with nets, and women pounded grain in wooden mortars before the houses.

In this village, with his wife and many children, lived a hunter by the name of Ogaloussa.

One morning Ogaloussa took his weapons down from the wall of his house and went into the forest to hunt. His wife and his children went to tend their fields, and drove their cattle out to graze. The day passed, and they ate their evening meal. Darkness came, but Ogaloussa didn't return.

Another day went by, and still Ogaloussa didn't come back. They talked about it and wondered what could have **detained** him. A week passed, then a month. Sometimes Ogaloussa's sons mentioned that he hadn't come home.

78

The family cared for the crops, and the sons hunted for game, but after a while they no longer talked about Ogaloussa.

Then one day, a few months after Ogaloussa's disappearance, another son was born to Ogaloussa's wife. His name was Puli. Puli grew older. He began to sit up and crawl. The time came when Puli began to talk, and the first thing he said was, "Where is my father?"

The other sons looked across the rice fields.

"Yes," one of them said. "Where is Father?"

"He should have returned long ago," another one said.

"Something must have happened. We ought to look for him," a third son said.

"He went into the forest, but where will we find him?" another one asked.

"I saw him go," one of them said. "He

went that way, across the river. Let us follow the trail and search for him."

So the sons took their weapons and started out to look for Ogaloussa. When they were deep among the great trees and vines of the forest they lost the trail. They searched in the forest until one of them found the trail again. They followed it until they lost the way once more, and then another son found the trail. It was dark in the forest, and many times they became lost. Each time another son found the way. At last they came to a clearing among the trees, and there on the ground scattered about lay Ogaloussa's bones and his rusted weapons. They knew then that Ogaloussa had been killed in the hunt.

One of the sons stepped forward and said, "I know how to put a dead person's bones together." He gathered all of Ogaloussa's bones and put them together, each in its right place.

Another son said, "I have knowledge too. I know how to cover the **skeleton** with sinews and flesh." He went to work, and he covered Ogaloussa's bones with sinews and flesh.

A third son said, "I have the power to put blood into a body." He went forward and put blood into Ogaloussa's veins, and then he stepped aside.

Another of the sons said, "I can put breath into a body." He did his work, and when he was through they saw Ogaloussa's chest rise and fall.

"I can give the power of movement to a body," another of them said. He put the power of movement into his father's body, and Ogaloussa sat up and opened his eyes.

"I can give him the power of speech," another son said. He gave the body the power of speech, and then he stepped back.

Ogaloussa looked around him. He stood up.

"Where are my weapons?" he asked.

They picked up his rusted weapons from the grass where they lay and gave them to him. They then returned the way they had come, through the forest and the rice fields, until they had arrived once more in the village.

Ogaloussa went into his house. His wife prepared a bath for him and he bathed. She prepared food for him and he ate. Four days he remained in the house, and on the fifth day he came out. He killed a cow for a great feast, then he took the cow's tail and braided it. He decorated the tail with

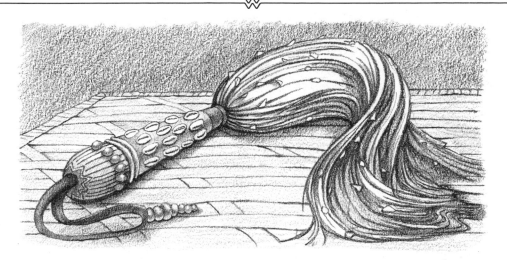

beads and shells and bits of shiny metal. It was a beautiful thing. Ogaloussa carried it with him to important affairs. When there was a dance or an important ceremony he always had it with him. The people of the village thought it was the most beautiful cow-tail switch they had ever seen.

Soon there was a celebration in the village because Ogaloussa had returned. The people dressed in their best clothes, the musicians brought out their instruments, and a big dance began. The drummers beat their drums and the women sang. Everyone was happy.

Ogaloussa carried his cow-tail switch, and everyone admired it. Some of the men came forward to Ogaloussa and asked for the cow-tail switch, but Ogaloussa kept it in his hand. Now and then there was a **clamor** and much confusion as many people asked for it at once. The women and children begged for it too, but Ogaloussa refused them all.

Finally he stood up to talk. The dancing stopped and people came close to hear what Ogaloussa had to say.

"A long time ago I went into the forest," Ogaloussa said. "While I was hunting I was killed by a leopard. Then my sons came for me. They brought me back to my village. I will give this cow-tail switch to one of my sons. All of them have done something to bring me back from the dead, but I have only one cow tail to give. I shall give it to the one who did the most to bring me home."

So an argument started.

"He will give it to me!" one of the sons said. "It was I who did the most, for I found the trail in the forest when it was lost!"

"No, he will give it to me!" another son said. "It was I who put his bones together!"

"It was I who covered his bones with sinews and flesh!" another said. "He will give it to me!"

"It was I who gave him the power of movement!" another son said. "I deserve it most!"

Another son said it was he who should have the switch, because he had put blood in Ogaloussa's veins. Another claimed it because he had put breath in the body. Each of the sons argued his right to **possess** the wonderful cow-tail switch.

Before long not only the sons but the other people of the village were talking. Some of them argued that the son who had put blood in Ogaloussa's veins should get the switch, others that the one who had given Ogaloussa's breath should get it. Some of them believed that all of the sons had done equal things, and that they should share it. They argued back and forth this way until Ogaloussa asked them to be quiet.

"To this son I will give the cow-tail switch, for I owe most to him," Ogaloussa said.

He came forward and bent low and handed it to—Puli, the little boy who had been born while Ogaloussa was in the forest!

The people of the village remembered then that the child's first words had been, "Where is my father?" They knew that Ogaloussa was right.

For there was a saying among them that a man is not really dead until he is forgotten.

SELECTING DETAILS FROM THE STORY.
Each of the following sentences helps
you understand the story. Complete each
sentence below by putting an *x* in the
box next to the correct answer.

1. After Ogaloussa had been gone for
   a long time, his sons
   ☐ a. asked about him every day.
   ☐ b. no longer talked about him.
   ☐ c. asked their friends and neighbors
   to look for him.

2. Ogaloussa's sons went into the forest to
   ☐ a. hunt animals for food.
   ☐ b. see which one of them was the
   bravest.
   ☐ c. search for their father.

3. Ogaloussa said that he had been
   killed by
   ☐ a. a leopard.
   ☐ b. another hunter.
   ☐ c. a falling tree.

4. Ogaloussa gave the cow-tail switch to
   the son who
   ☐ a. put his bones together.
   ☐ b. gave him the power of speech.
   ☐ c. asked where his father was.

HANDLING STORY ELEMENTS. Each of
the following questions reviews your
understanding of story elements. Put
an *x* in the box next to the correct
answer to each question.

1. What happened first in the *plot* of
   "The Cow-Tail Switch"?
   ☐ a. Ogaloussa made a beautiful cow-
   tail switch.
   ☐ b. Puli asked, "Where is my father?"
   ☐ c. One son gave Ogaloussa's body
   the power of movement.

2. Who is the *main character* in the story?
   ☐ a. Ogaloussa
   ☐ b. Ogaloussa's wife
   ☐ c. Puli

3. "The Cow-Tail Switch" is *set* in
   ☐ a. a busy city.
   ☐ b. a large town.
   ☐ c. a village in Liberia.

4. Which statement best tells the *theme*
   of the story?
   ☐ a. A father's decision reminds
   everyone that a person is
   not dead until that person
   is forgotten.
   ☐ b. When a man returns after
   disappearing, the joyful people
   hold a celebration.
   ☐ c. It is dangerous to go hunting
   alone in a forest.

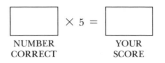

NUMBER   YOUR
CORRECT   SCORE

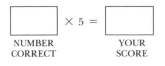

NUMBER   YOUR
CORRECT   SCORE

OBSERVING NEW VOCABULARY WORDS. Answer the following vocabulary questions by putting an *x* in the box next to the correct answer. The vocabulary words are printed in **boldface** in the story. If you wish, look back at the words before you answer the questions.

1. When Ogaloussa didn't return to his home, his family wondered what could have detained him. The word *detained* means
   ☐ a. delayed.
   ☐ b. tricked.
   ☐ c. protected.

2. Each son thought that he deserved to possess the wonderful cow-tail switch. As used here, the word *possess* means
   ☐ a. touch.
   ☐ b. sell.
   ☐ c. own.

3. One son knew how to cover the skeleton with flesh. Which expression best defines the word *skeleton*?
   ☐ a. powerful muscles
   ☐ b. a kind of clothing
   ☐ c. the frame of bones in a body

4. There was a clamor and much confusion as many people asked for the cow-tail switch. What is the meaning of the word *clamor*?
   ☐ a. a moment of silence
   ☐ b. a loud noise
   ☐ c. a full meal

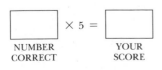

NUMBER CORRECT × 5 = YOUR SCORE

COMPLETING A CLOZE PASSAGE. Complete the following paragraph by filling in each blank with one of the words listed in the box below. Each of the words appears in the story. Since there are five words and four blanks, one word in the group will not be used.

With an area of _____ 1

12,000,000 square miles, Africa is

the second largest continent. The

Sahara, the largest desert in the

world, is _____ in Africa. 2

It _____ more than one quarter 3

of the continent. Africa also contains the

Nile, the world's longest river. It flows from

Lake Victoria to the Mediterranean Sea,

a _____ of about 4,150 miles. 4

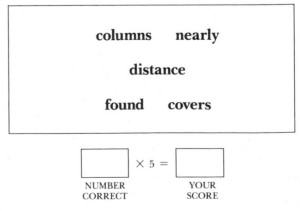

columns   nearly

distance

found   covers

NUMBER CORRECT × 5 = YOUR SCORE

84

KNOWING HOW TO READ CRITICALLY. Each of the following questions will help you to think critically about the selection. Put an *x* in the box next to the correct answer.

1. Which statement is true?
   - ☐ a. When Ogaloussa didn't come home, his sons went to look for him that day.
   - ☐ b. All of Ogaloussa's sons did something to bring their father back.
   - ☐ c. Very few of the villagers admired the cow-tail switch.

2. Which son did Ogaloussa give the cow-tail switch to?
   - ☐ a. the youngest son
   - ☐ b. the oldest son
   - ☐ c. the strongest son

3. After Ogaloussa told the people the reason for his decision, everyone
   - ☐ a. wondered if he had made the right choice.
   - ☐ b. thought he had acted foolishly.
   - ☐ c. understood and agreed.

4. One important point that this story makes is that
   - ☐ a. if you act selfishly, you will never receive a beautiful gift.
   - ☐ b. it is difficult to follow a trail in the forest when it is dark.
   - ☐ c. when you treasure the memory of a person, that person never really dies.

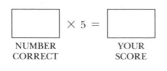

NUMBER
CORRECT

× 5 =

YOUR
SCORE

Questions for Writing and Discussion

- Should Ogaloussa have given the cow-tail switch to Puli—or should he have chosen another son? Explain your answer.
- In speaking to his sons, Ogaloussa said, "All of them have done something to bring me back." In fact, they did at least *eight* different things. How many of these can you list?
- Read the last sentence of the story again. What does it mean? Do you agree? Why?

Use the boxes below to total your scores for the exercises. Then write your score on pages 150 and 151.

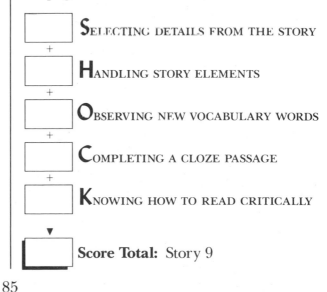

SELECTING DETAILS FROM THE STORY

+

HANDLING STORY ELEMENTS

+

OBSERVING NEW VOCABULARY WORDS

+

COMPLETING A CLOZE PASSAGE

+

KNOWING HOW TO READ CRITICALLY

▼

Score Total: Story 9

10

The Snakes of Bera

by Cecelia Rathbone

I guess we have no choice—we'll *have* to land," Captain Grace DeLauria sighed, unhappily.

"I suppose so," replied Lieutenant Fred Asquith, shaking his head. "What an assignment—Bera, the dullest planet in the universe!"

The two members of the Galactic Space Patrol had attempted, unsuccessfully, to get out of this task. Bera was the smallest planet in the galaxy. It had been discovered way back at the end of the twenty-first century, and space explorers had visited it just once. Most of their report had been lost when the planet Earth exploded during the last interplanetary war. What was left in the report did not promise much excitement.

According to the account, the Berans were gentle and harmless. At that point in time, they were still so backward that they had no machines. Photographs from space suggested that little had changed on Bera over the years. But the thick clouds that surrounded the planet made it impossible to tell. Recently, there had been a series of **violent** explosions on nearby Pluto. It was likely that the fallout had damaged Bera. Only through human exploration could they know for sure.

"Living species may have died out in the last year," the Space Patrol commander had said. "There may have been floods, or fires, or earthquakes on the planet. Your mission is to find out if the Berans need help. If they do, we will send assistance."

The young Space Patrollers would have preferred the bright lights of the cities of Venus. They had hoped to experience some of the excitement of Mars.

Grace sighed again, reached over and pushed the LAND button on the control panel. Instantly, the little spacecraft began to **descend**. When they felt the familiar jolt which meant they had touched down, Fred pushed the POWER OFF button. Then he and Grace unbuckled their safety belts and stood up to stretch.

Grace checked the laser gun at the belt of her gold-colored space suit. She pulled her communicator out of a pocket and flipped it on. With it in operation, she could understand and be understood in any language in the universe.

"Well," Grace said, "we may as well get it over with. Let's see what we can find."

They stepped out of the little craft onto a large plain of pale pink grass. In the white sky, a green sun shone hot and high. Suddenly, across the plain of grass, a dozen creatures were marching directly toward them.

They were all extremely tall and walked on two legs like Earthlings. They seemed to have hands, for they carried long spears. As they drew closer, Grace and Fred could see that they had handsome, near-human faces. But they wore no clothing, for their bodies were covered with thick, shaggy fur which ranged in color from purple to white.

Grace put one hand on her laser gun. As she did, she could hear the buzz of the communicator in her pocket. One of the creatures stepped forward. Its hair was pale, and it shone a bright green in the sunlight. The face seemed intelligent and wise—but sad.

"We greet you," the Beran said. The words sputtered through the machine as if spoken in English. The voice was gentle and deep.

"We greet you as well," Grace answered. "We come from another world," she went on. "We want you to know that we are your friends. We have come to see what is here and to learn what you may need."

"I believe you," said the Beran. "We will show you. After you see, you will understand."

Suddenly, Grace and Fred found themselves in the midst of a crowd of

Berans. Hairy hands with long fingers **wrenched** the laser guns from their belts. Then the hands were on their arms, pushing them gently but firmly forward.

It was not a long walk, but the green sun was blazing hot. Pink and gray fields stretched along the rough road. Grace did not recognize the strange crops she saw in the fields, but she realized they were dying. "Probably caused by the fallout from Pluto," she thought.

From crude huts, Berans of all ages came out to stare at the newcomers. The Berans were very thin, and some of the furry youngsters had the puffed-up stomachs of starving children.

Waterwheels slowly turned in streams that were almost dry. Surprisingly, all along the road Grace and Fred saw carvings—of snakes! The curved carvings were amazingly true to life, each with scales, a tail, and forked tongue. Now and then one could see the carving of a skin, as though it had been shed. Some of the skins were painted blue.

One of the Berans pointed at a carving and said, "The snakes were our good fortune. We make these carvings to honor them. We beg the sun that they will return to us one day."

The Beran touched a bag that hung from its furry throat, saying, "This contains one of their dear blue skins. If the snakes were to return, even for an hour, they would bring us life again. But they do not return." Grace saw that the hairy face was wet with tears.

The Space Patrollers were weary and thirsty when they finally stopped. Then they were pushed into a large stone hut. In the center stood a huge carving of a snake, a carving so real that the patrollers jumped back upon seeing it, momentarily startled.

The pale-faced Beran who had greeted them followed Fred and Grace into the hut.

"We deeply regret what must be done," said the Beran in a sorrowful voice. "You are in the room of the Dear Snake. Once our country was rich in snakes. They were our helpers. To kill a snake was our most serious crime. While the snakes were here, we were happy. We had plenty of food and pure water. Our children did not swell up and die."

The Beran touched the bag around its neck. "Now, in memory of the snakes, we wear the skins they have shed. That is all we have left."

The Beran seemed thoughtful. "We do not know the reason the snakes left us—but they are gone. And our water has gone, too. There is no more rain. Our streams have dried up. Even our great river is so low that we can walk upon the bottom. Our crops are dying. We have very little food."

The Beran stared sadly at Fred and Grace. "Now every drop of water, every crumb of food, is precious. We cannot give water or food to strangers. We cannot support even one more life."

The Beran paused for a moment, then said very softly, "Perhaps you are good. But we cannot let you live."

Grace and Fred looked at each other, shocked.

"Take us back to the carrier that brought us," said Grace. "We will leave you. We will eat and drink nothing. We will tell others of your trouble. We will send you help."

The Beran shook its head. "The great bird that brought you here must die, too. It will need food and water before it can fly again. We cannot spare food and water."

"No, no," cried Fred. "You don't understand! It is not a *living* bird! It needs no food!"

The Beran looked even sadder. "Of course you must say that. You wish to save your lives. We are sorry, but we must destroy you. Do not fear. Your death will be painless."

The Beran turned. "Now I will leave you for a time. You must find peace within yourselves."

With that the Beran walked out of the stone room. It was very quiet outside, but Grace and Fred knew that they were being guarded by a dozen Berans.

For a long time the patrollers said nothing. The room seemed to be closing in on them. The heat suddenly was stifling.

"It's so warm in here," said Grace. She unzipped the gold space suit. Under it she wore the blue jumpsuit that was part of the Space Patrol uniform. She sat down on the stone floor, dropping the space suit beside her.

Fred unzipped the collar of his own space suit. The blue turtleneck of the jumpsuit showed against the gold.

"It's . . . unbelievable," muttered Fred. "We thought this was going to be such a dull trip. And now," his voice began to choke, "it's going to be . . . our last."

They sat in silence. Too soon the door opened and the pale-haired Beran, holding a cup, entered the room.

"You must drink from this—" began the Beran. Then the Beran's eyes widened in shock. The cup fell and shattered on the stone floor. A green liquid spread over the ground, but the Beran did not see it. The Beran fell to its knees.

"You—you are dear snakes—" the Beran said hoarsely. "You have come again—you have come to help us—"

Grace did not understand what the Beran was saying, but she realized that this was their chance.

"Yes," she said. She quickly stood up, and Fred rose, too. "We have come to tell you," said Grace, "that help is on the way. You must let us go back on the bird that brought us. You—you have not—killed it?"

"No, no, not yet, oh Great One," the Beran said. "Go—go—do what you will." The Beran stood up, bowed low, and walked backward through the open doorway. Outside, the Beran called out to the guards.

"Sons and daughters, we have been honored once more! They are snakes!" The Beran raised its arms and sang out to the green sun. "Life—they bring life!"

Grace picked up her space suit and stepped from the stone building. The guards dropped their spears and fell to their knees, touching their furry foreheads to the ground. Fred and Grace made their way through the crowd of bent, hairy backs.

"This way," Fred said. They turned in the direction they had been taken. In the distance, across the pink plain, they could see the spacecraft.

Back inside the ship, Grace switched on the controls and the craft swiftly began to rise. Moments later, they leaned back in their seats and breathed deeply and gratefully.

"What was that all about?" asked Fred. "Why did they say we were snakes and then let us go?"

Grace laughed. "I think I know what happened," she said. "The Berans don't wear clothes—they have animal fur. They don't even know what clothing is. I took off my space suit. Only *snakes* shed their skins!"

Suddenly, over the faint sound of the engines, the patrollers heard a clap of thunder. They looked out the portholes. The white sky of Bera had darkened, and the green sun had dropped behind a purple cloud. Heavy rain was pouring down, soaking the pink grass, **drenching** the planet of Bera.

Grace gasped.

"Because they believed in us?" she wondered.

"Maybe," Fred said. "Or perhaps the exhaust cloud from our spaceship stirred up the atmosphere."

Grace adjusted the craft's telescope and peered down. Through the sheets of rain, she could see a thousand furry hands reaching upward. She half believed that she could hear chants, chants of thanks to the blue snakes from the sky.

SELECTING DETAILS FROM THE STORY.
Each of the following sentences helps
you understand the story. Complete each
sentence below by putting an *x* in the
box next to the correct answer.

1. Grace and Fred were sent to Bera to
   find out if the Berans
   - ☐ a. were dangerous.
   - ☐ b. were intelligent.
   - ☐ c. needed help.

2. The Berans believed that snakes
   brought them
   - ☐ a. bad luck.
   - ☐ b. food and pure water.
   - ☐ c. beautiful carvings.

3. At the end of the story, the Berans
   - ☐ a. pushed the Space Patrollers into
     the spaceship and warned them
     never to return.
   - ☐ b. fell to their knees and let the
     patrollers leave.
   - ☐ c. begged the patrollers to stay.

4. Fred thought it might have started to
   rain because the
   - ☐ a. exhaust from the spaceship
     stirred up the atmosphere.
   - ☐ b. Berans believed that he and
     Grace were snakes.
   - ☐ c. climate on Bera was changing.

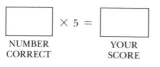

NUMBER
CORRECT   × 5 =   YOUR
SCORE

HANDLING STORY ELEMENTS. Each of
the following questions reviews your
understanding of story elements. Put
an *x* in the box next to the correct
answer to each question.

1. What happened last in the *plot* of
   the story?
   - ☐ a. Grace and Fred saw carvings of
     snakes along the road.
   - ☐ b. The Space Patrollers heard a clap
     of thunder, and the sky grew dark.
   - ☐ c. A Beran ordered the patrollers
     to drink from a cup.

2. Which sentence best *characterizes*
   the Berans?
   - ☐ a. They were short and stout.
   - ☐ b. They looked like human beings,
     but they walked on four legs.
   - ☐ c. They were tall and thin with
     thick, shaggy fur.

3. "The Snakes of Bera" is *set*
   - ☐ a. in the past.
   - ☐ b. in the future.
   - ☐ c. at the present time.

4. Which sentence best tells the *theme* of
   the story?
   - ☐ a. The lives of two space patrollers
     are threatened and then saved
     because of snakes.
   - ☐ b. Two space explorers are not eager
     to visit a planet named Bera.
   - ☐ c. Two space patrollers are locked
     in a stone hut on the planet Bera.

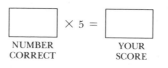

NUMBER
CORRECT   × 5 =   YOUR
SCORE

OBSERVING NEW VOCABULARY WORDS. Answer the following vocabulary questions by putting an *x* in the box next to the correct answer. The vocabulary words are printed in **boldface** in the story. If you wish, look back at the words before you answer the questions.

1. Hairy hands with long fingers wrenched the guns from their belts. What is the meaning of the word *wrenched*?
   ☐ a. placed carefully
   ☐ b. pulled sharply
   ☐ c. patted gently

2. Violent explosions on Pluto may have caused damaged to Bera. The word *violent* means
   ☐ a. very rough and forceful.
   ☐ b. excellent or outstanding.
   ☐ c. simple or easy.

3. When Grace pushed the LAND button, the spacecraft began to descend. What is the meaning of the word *descend*?
   ☐ a. wobble or shake
   ☐ b. go up or rise
   ☐ c. go down or drop

4. Heavy rains poured down, soaking the grass, drenching the planet. Which of the following best defines (gives the meaning of) the word *drenching*?
   ☐ a. hitting everywhere
   ☐ b. missing totally
   ☐ c. wetting completely

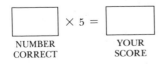

NUMBER CORRECT   YOUR SCORE

COMPLETING A CLOZE PASSAGE. Complete the following paragraph by filling in each blank with one of the words listed in the box below. Each of the words appears in the story. Since there are five words and four blanks, one word in the group will not be used.

Snakes grow a new _____ $_1$

at least twice a year. To do that, the snake

must first _____ its old skin. $_2$

The _____ simply slips out of $_3$

its skin by turning it inside out. This is

a little like removing a glove by pulling

it _____ out over your hand. $_4$

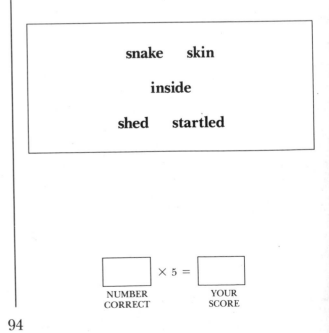

snake   skin

inside

shed   startled

NUMBER CORRECT   YOUR SCORE

KNOWING HOW TO READ CRITICALLY. Each of the following questions will help you to think critically about the selection. Put an *x* in the box next to the correct answer.

1. Why did the Berans believe that Grace and Fred were snakes?
   □ a. The Berans thought that Grace's space suit was skin that she shed.
   □ b. The Berans suddenly realized that the patrollers had magical powers.
   □ c. The patrollers cleverly fooled them into believing they were snakes.

2. The cup that the Beran offered to Grace and Fred probably contained
   □ a. water.
   □ b. juice.
   □ c. poison.

3. When the Berans saw the rain, they were probably
   □ a. afraid.
   □ b. thrilled.
   □ c. sad.

4. Which statement is true?
   □ a. The patrollers thought that Bera would be dull, but that didn't prove to be the case.
   □ b. The weather on Bera was usually cloudy and cold.
   □ c. The Berans wore brightly colored, attractive clothing.

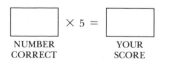

×5 =

NUMBER CORRECT   YOUR SCORE

Questions for Writing and Discussion
- List at least four ways in which the Berans honored snakes.
- Colors play an important part in "The Snakes of Bera." Find as many examples as you can to support that statement. Explain fully.
- According to one account, the Berans were gentle, harmless, and backward. How do you think Grace and Fred will describe the Berans when they write their report?

Use the boxes below to total your scores for the exercises. Then write your score on pages 150 and 151.

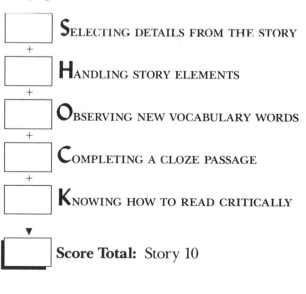

SELECTING DETAILS FROM THE STORY

+

HANDLING STORY ELEMENTS

+

OBSERVING NEW VOCABULARY WORDS

+

COMPLETING A CLOZE PASSAGE

+

KNOWING HOW TO READ CRITICALLY

▼

Score Total: Story 10

II

Of Missing Persons

by Jack Finney

*W*alk *in as though it were an ordinary travel agency,* the stranger I'd met had told me. *Ask a few ordinary questions—about a trip you're planning, a vacation, something like that. Then hint about The Folder. But whatever you do, don't mention it directly. Wait till he brings it up himself. And if he doesn't, you might as well forget it. Because you'll never see it. That's all.*

I rehearsed it all in my mind, over and over. But I felt like a fool, searching the storefronts for the street number I'd memorized. It was the noon hour, West 42nd Street, New York, rainy and windy. The world was real and drab, and this was hopeless.

Anyway, I thought, who am I to see The Folder, even if there is one? I could hear myself telling the travel agent, "My name is Charley Ewell. I'm a young guy who works in a bank, a teller. I don't like the job, I don't make much money, and I never will. I've lived in New York for more than three years and haven't many friends. I see more movies than I want to, and I'm sick of meals alone in restaurants. I have ordinary abilities, looks, and thoughts. Do I qualify?"

Now I spotted the address. It was an old office building, tired, outdated. I pushed through the doors into the tiny lobby. On the little wall directory with twenty names, I found "Acme Travel Agency." Then I pressed the bell for the elevator and rode upstairs. As I did I thought to myself, "This is crazy. This is insane."

Upstairs the office was bright and clean. Behind a counter stood a tall, gray-haired man. He had a telephone at his ear. He glanced up, nodded to beckon me in, and I felt my heart pounding. Yes, he was the man, all right— he fit the description exactly!

Standing before him now, I waited, leaning on the counter. I looked around. It seemed just like any ordinary travel agency with posters on the walls and racks full of folders. Again I felt like a fool.

"Can I help you?" the tall, gray-haired man asked, smiling at me, and suddenly I was terribly nervous.

"Yes. I'd like to . . . to . . . get away." *You fool,* I told myself, *Don't rush it!* I watched him closely to see what effect my answer had had, but he didn't flick an eyelash.

"Well, there are lots of places to go," he said politely. From under the counter he took a folder and handed it to me. "FLY TO BUENOS AIRES," it said in large green letters across the top.

I looked at it long enough to be polite. Then I shook my head. I was afraid to talk, afraid I'd say the wrong thing.

"Something quieter, maybe?" he asked, handing me another folder. It said, "VISIT THE FORESTS OF MAINE." He reached for a third folder as he said, "Bermuda is nice."

I decided to risk it. "No," I said, and shook my head. "What I'm really looking for is a permanent place. A new place to live in and settle down in— forever." I stared directly into his eyes. "I mean—for the rest of my life."

He smiled pleasantly and said, "What are you looking for? What do you want?"

I held my breath, then said it. "Escape."

"From what?"

"Well . . ." Now I hesitated. I'd never put it into words before. "I want to get away from this city—from cities in general. From worry. From loneliness. And fear. And the things I read in my newspapers." And then I couldn't stop talking, the words spilling out. "From never doing what I really want to do or having much fun. From modern life itself—at least the way it is today." I looked straight at him and said softly, "I want to get away from the world."

He lowered his gaze to look into my eyes and said, "Do you like people? Tell the truth, because I'll know if you don't."

"Yes. It isn't easy for me to relax, though, and be myself, and make friends."

He nodded and smiled. "You know," he said casually, "we occasionally get people in here who seem to be looking for pretty much the kind of place you want. So just as a sort of little joke . . ."

I couldn't breathe. This is what I was told he would say if he thought I was okay.

"We've printed a little folder. Simply for our own amusement, you understand—and for occasional clients like you. You'll have to look at it *here* if you're interested. It's not the sort of thing we'd care to have the public, in general, know about."

I whispered hoarsely, "I'm interested."

He handed me a long thin folder. The cover was dark blue, the color of a night sky. Across the top in white letters it said, "VISIT ENCHANTING VERNA!" The blue cover was sprinkled with stars. Just under the word "Verna" was a star larger and brighter than the others, and across the bottom of the cover it said, "Verna, where life is the way it *should* be."

I opened the folder, which was beautifully printed. The pictures looked very real. I mean in one picture you could see dew glistening on the grass, and it actually looked wet. In another, human faces seemed about to speak.

I studied a large picture spreading across two pages. You saw a rolling valley and slopes covered with forest, and the color was beautiful, perfect. There were miles of green, **majestic** trees, and you knew as you stared at that forest-covered valley, that this was the way America looked when it was new. And you knew that every stream ran pure, and if you could breathe in that air, it would be sweeter than the air you were breathing now.

Another picture showed eight people on a yellow beach. They were talking, and the sun was bright, and you *knew* that they liked their work, all of them, whatever it was, as well as their **leisure time**, too.

I'd never seen anything like their faces before. They were ordinary enough in looks, the people in that picture—more or less familiar types, of various ages. But you knew that these people were *happy*. You knew that they'd *been* happy, day after day for a long, long time—and that they always would be, and they knew it.

I wanted to join them so much I could hardly stand it. I looked up at the man behind the counter and said, "This is—very interesting."

"Yes. We've had customers so interested, so carried away, that they didn't want to talk about anything else." He laughed. "They actually wanted to know rates, details, everything."

I nodded to show I understood and that I agreed with them. "And I suppose you've worked out a whole story to go with this?" I glanced at the folder in my hand.

"Oh, yes. What would you like to know?"

"These people," I said softly, "what do they do?"

"They work. Everyone does. They simply live their lives doing what they like. They work at whatever it is they really want to do."

"And if there isn't anything they really want to do?"

He shook his head. "There is always something, for everyone, that a person really wants to do. It's just that here there is rarely time to find out what it is. Life is simple there, and it's peaceful, serene. Distances are small, and people live and work in small communities. They raise or make most of the things they use. There is a great deal of visiting and sharing of meals and sports of all kinds. There is no pressure to make lots of money, and there is no crime. Every man, woman, and child is a happy person."

I looked at the folder and turned a page. Homes there seemed simple, but beautiful and comfortable in their way. You knew as you looked at them that these rooms were *home,* really home, to the people who lived in them.

"Who are you?" I asked the man, staring into his eyes.

"We—that is to say, the people of Verna, are people like yourself. Verna is a planet very much like this one, and we are people like you. But our history and development have been quite different from yours."

He smiled. "Amusing fantasy, isn't it?"

"Yes. And where is Verna?"

"Light years away, by your measurements."

"A little hard to get to then, wouldn't it be?"

For a moment he looked at me. Then he turned toward the window and stared out. "All I can tell you," he said, "is that we travel through space in a very special way—a way that takes almost no time at all." He smiled again. "Why, it is possible to draw in a breath here on Earth—and **exhale** it on Verna."

I leaned across the counter and nodded. "I like your little joke," I said. "I like it very much, more than I can possibly tell you." Very softly I added, "When does it stop being a joke?"

For a moment he studied me. Then he spoke. "Now. If you want it to."

You've got to decide on the spot, the stranger had told me, *because you'll never get another chance. I know. I've tried.*

Now I stood there thinking. There were some people I'd hate never to see again—and this was the world that I'd been born in. Then I thought about going back to my job, and returning to my room at night. I thought of the green valley in the picture and the yellow beach in the morning sun. "I'll go," I whispered. "If you'll have me."

"Be sure," he said sharply. "Be certain. If you have the least doubt . . ."

"I'm sure," I said.

The gray-haired man opened a drawer under the counter and took out a yellow ticket. The printing on it said, "Good for ONE TRIP TO VERNA. One-way only."

"Ah—how much is it?" I said, reaching for my wallet.

"Whatever you've got with you." He smiled, "You won't need money any more, and we can use it here for office costs."

"I don't have much," I said.

"That doesn't matter."

He stamped the ticket and handed it to me. It said, "Good this day only," followed by the date.

I put $11.17 on the counter—two five-dollar bills, a one, and seventeen cents.

"Take this ticket to the Acme Bus Station," the gray-haired man said. Then he gave me directions.

It's a tiny hole in the wall, the Acme Bus Station—just a little storefront, really.

You could pass it a thousand times and never see it. When I arrived, a man stood behind the counter working on some papers. The man glanced up as I stepped in, looked toward my hand for my ticket, and when I showed it, nodded at the last chair.

I sat down and looked around at the other people who were waiting there silently. There was a young woman, her hands folded on her purse. There was a young man in work clothes, his wife beside him holding their little girl in her lap. And there was a man of about fifty, his face staring out into the rain. He was wearing very expensive clothes. He could have been the vice-president of a large bank, I thought, and wondered what his ticket had cost.

After twenty minutes, a small, battered old bus pulled up at the curb outside. We got on board and the bus began to make its way through traffic.

Each of us sat staring out the rain-splattered windows. After a while I dozed, and when I awoke we were turning off the highway onto a muddy road. Then the bus slowed, and we were parked beside what looked like a barn.

It *was* a barn—the driver walked up to it, pulled the big sliding wood door open and stood holding it open as we filed in. Then he released it and the big door slid closed of its own weight. The barn was damp and old and it smelled of cattle. The driver pointed a flashlight beam at an old wooden bench. "Sit here, please," he said quietly. "Get your tickets ready." He moved down the line, punching each of our tickets. Then he was at the door again, sliding it open just enough for him to pass through.

For a moment we saw him against the night sky. "Good luck," he said. "Just wait where you are."

He released the door. It slid closed, cutting off the beam of his flashlight. A moment later we heard the motor start, and the bus lumbered away.

The dark barn was silent now, except for our breathing. Time ticked away, and I felt the urge to speak to whoever was next to me. But I didn't quite know what to say, and I began to feel embarrassed, a little foolish. I was very aware that I was simply sitting in an old and deserted barn.

The seconds passed and I moved my feet restlessly. Presently I realized that I was getting cold and chilled. Then suddenly I *knew*—and I was filled with anger and shame. We'd been tricked—cheated out of our money by our desperate desire to find happiness! We'd listened to that absurd and fantastic fable, and now we would sit there until we finally came to our senses. How could I have been foolish enough to believe anything so ridiculous!

Suddenly I was on my feet, stumbling across the wooden floor. The big barn door was heavier than I'd thought, but I slid it back. Then I took a running step outside, and turned to shout back to the others to come along.

As I turned, the inside of that barn came alive with light. Through its dust-covered windows streamed the light of a brilliant blue and sunny sky. And, suddenly, the air in my lungs, as I opened my mouth to shout, was sweeter than any air I had ever breathed in my life.

Through the dusty window, in less than the blink of an eye, I caught a glimpse of that tree-covered valley, and a patch of sun-drenched beach. And then the heavy door slid shut, despite my desperate effort to stop it. And I was standing alone in a cold and rain-swept night.

It took me four or five seconds to pull the door open again. But that was four or five seconds too long. The barn was empty and dark. There was nothing inside but a worn pine bench. There was no one inside now, but

I knew where they'd gone. They were walking, laughing aloud, in that green forest valley.

I work at a job I don't like, and I ride to it in the subway reading the daily newspaper, the bad news it contains. I live in a rented room, and on my dresser is a little yellow ticket. Printed on it are the words "Good for ONE TRIP TO VERNA," and stamped on the back is a date. But the date is long since gone, the ticket punched and **void**.

I've been back to the Acme Travel Agency. The first time, the tall gray-haired gentleman walked up to me and put two five-dollar bills, a one, and seventeen cents in front of me. "You left this on the counter the last time you were here," he said looking me squarely in the eyes. Then he added, "I don't know why." Some customers came in and he turned to greet them. There was nothing for me to do but leave.

Walk in as though it were an ordinary travel agency. Ask a few ordinary questions—about a trip you're planning, a vacation, something like that. Then hint about The Folder. But don't mention it directly. Give him time to offer it himself. And if he does, then make up your mind—and stick to it! Because you won't ever get a second chance. I know, because I've tried. And tried. And tried.

SELECTING DETAILS FROM THE STORY.
Each of the following sentences helps
you understand the story. Complete each
sentence below by putting an *x* in the
box next to the correct answer.

1. Charley Ewell told the travel agent that
   he wanted to
   ☐ a. take a vacation in Maine.
   ☐ b. travel around the world.
   ☐ c. escape.

2. In Verna, people lived
   ☐ a. simple, peaceful, happy lives.
   ☐ b. in fancy houses filled with
         modern inventions.
   ☐ c. in fear of poverty and crime.

3. The travel agent opened a drawer and
   gave Charley a
   ☐ a. round-trip ticket to Verna.
   ☐ b. one-way ticket to Verna.
   ☐ c. letter admitting Charley to Verna.

4. Charley ran out of the barn, and as
   the barn door slid shut behind him,
   he saw
   ☐ a. the travel agent smiling at him.
   ☐ b. the blue folder that said,
         "Visit Verna."
   ☐ c. a tree-covered valley and a patch
         of beach.

HANDLING STORY ELEMENTS. Each of
the following questions reviews your
understanding of story elements. Put
an *x* in the box next to the correct
answer to each question.

1. What happened first in the *plot* of
   "Of Missing Persons"?
   ☐ a. Charley searched the storefronts
         for the street number the
         stranger had given him.
   ☐ b. The travel agent returned $11.17
         to Charley.
   ☐ c. The bus driver moved down the
         line, punching everyone's ticket.

2. Which group of words best *characterizes*
   Charley Ewell?
   ☐ a. cheerful; confident; wealthy
   ☐ b. lonely; young; unhappy
   ☐ c. popular; fearless; pleased

3. What is the *mood* of "Of Missing
   Persons"?
   ☐ a. joyous
   ☐ b. terrifying
   ☐ c. sad

4. Which sentence best tells the *theme* of
   the story?
   ☐ a. Travel agents know about
         interesting and unusual places.
   ☐ b. It can be difficult to make friends
         in a large, bustling city.
   ☐ c. When a young man acts hastily,
         he loses a once in a lifetime
         opportunity.

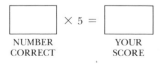

× 5 =

NUMBER
CORRECT

YOUR
SCORE

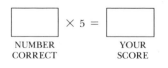

× 5 =

NUMBER
CORRECT

YOUR
SCORE

OBSERVING NEW VOCABULARY WORDS. Answer the following vocabulary questions by putting an *x* in the box next to the correct answer. The vocabulary words are printed in **boldface** in the story. If you wish, look back at the words before you answer the questions.

1. He said it was possible to draw in a breath here on Earth and exhale it on Verna. The word *exhale* means
   □ a. save.
   □ b. increase.
   □ c. breathe out.

2. Charley could tell that on Verna people liked their work and their leisure time, too. The expression *leisure time* means time when one is
   □ a. extremely busy.
   □ b. not busy, or free.
   □ c. troubled or upset.

3. The forest was covered with miles of green, majestic trees. The word *majestic* means
   □ a. pale and colorless.
   □ b. grand and splendid.
   □ c. ruined and damaged.

4. The date had passed, so Charley could no longer use the ticket; it was punched and void. The word *void* means
   □ a. too expensive.
   □ b. difficult to read.
   □ c. not in effect or useless.

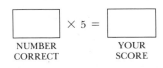

NUMBER CORRECT   × 5 =   YOUR SCORE

COMPLETING A CLOZE PASSAGE. Complete the following paragraph by filling in each blank with one of the words listed in the box below. Each of the words appears in the story. Since there are five words and four blanks, one word in the group will not be used.

Some people use _____₁

posters to decorate the walls of their

office. These colorful _____₂

are large, bright, and very attractive.

Usually, they can be obtained free of

charge from local travel _____₃.

Then, depending on how much one wishes

to spend, the posters can be mounted

on cardboard, framed, or placed

_____₄ on the wall.

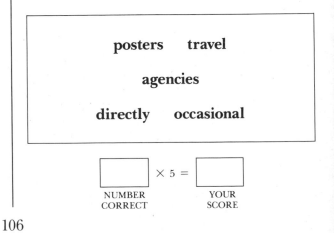

| posters | travel |
| agencies |
| directly | occasional |

NUMBER CORRECT   × 5 =   YOUR SCORE

KNOWING HOW TO READ CRITICALLY. Each of the following questions will help you to think critically about the selection. Put an *x* in the box next to the correct answer.

1. Clues in the story suggest that the travel agent
   - ☐ a. didn't like Verna.
   - ☐ b. knew very little about Verna.
   - ☐ c. came from Verna.

2. In what way were Charley and the stranger he'd met alike?
   - ☐ a. Each gave the travel agent $11.17.
   - ☐ b. Each wasted a chance to get to Verna.
   - ☐ c. Each worked as a teller in a bank.

3. When Charley was in the barn, he thought the travel agent had cheated him because the
   - ☐ a. travel agency looked unlike any agency Charley had ever seen.
   - ☐ b. agent had acted so suspiciously.
   - ☐ c. agent had asked for and had received all of Charley's money.

4. At the end of the story, Charley must have felt
   - ☐ a. disappointed.
   - ☐ b. satisfied.
   - ☐ c. very hopeful.

Questions for Writing and Discussion
- The word *vernal* means "having to do with spring." In your opinion, why did the author decide to call the planet "Verna"? Do you think it is a fitting name? Explain.
- Suppose that you were telling a friend about Charley Ewell. How would you describe him? If you could speak to Charley, what advice or suggestions would you give him?
- Who are the "missing persons" in the title of the story? Try to give two possible explanations.

Use the boxes below to total your scores for the exercises. Then write your score on pages 150 and 151.

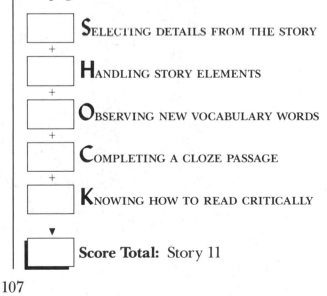

SELECTING DETAILS FROM THE STORY

+

HANDLING STORY ELEMENTS

+

OBSERVING NEW VOCABULARY WORDS

+

COMPLETING A CLOZE PASSAGE

+

KNOWING HOW TO READ CRITICALLY

▼

Score Total: Story 11

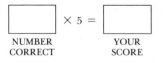

☐ × 5 = ☐

NUMBER
CORRECT

YOUR
SCORE

12

Matrimony Inn

by Lin Yutang

Wei Ku wanted to find the right woman to be his wife, but so far he had not been successful. In the year 807, he was traveling to Singho, and he stopped at an inn outside the city. Someone had suggested a marriage with a daughter of the famous Pam family. The matchmaker[1] had made an appointment to meet Wei at the temple at dawn.

Wei was pleased and excited by the possibility of marrying a woman who was so highly thought of. He was unable to sleep and got up long before dawn.

He dressed and washed and went to keep his appointment. A thin moon was shining in the sky, for it was still before daybreak. When he arrived at the place, Wei found an old man sitting on the steps of the temple. The man was reading a book by the light of the pale moon. A small bag lay on the floor by his side.

Wei Ku was curious about what the old man was reading at that early hour. Wei looked over his shoulders and found it was writing he could not understand. Wei was very well educated. He had studied all the ancient and modern languages, but he could not make out what this writing was.

"May I ask what language that is you are reading, old uncle?" said Wei.

---

1. **matchmaker:** a person who arranges, or tries to arrange, marriages for others.

"I thought I knew every kind of writing on earth, but I have never seen one like this."

"Of course you have not," answered the old man with a smile. "It is not written in any language that you would know."

"Then what is it?"

"You are a **mortal**," said the old man, "and this is a book of the spirit world."

"So you are a spirit! What are you doing here?"

"Why shouldn't I be here? You are out early, too. I have certain responsibilities to take care of on earth. I must go around during the night to check up on the people whose matters are my concern."

"What matters?" asked Wei.

"Matrimony," said the old man. "Marriage."

"Marriage!" said Wei Ku, greatly interested. "You are the very person I need to consult. I have never been successful in finding the right woman from a suitable family to be my wife. In fact, I have come here this morning to keep an appointment concerning a daughter of the Pam family who is said to be very intelligent, attractive, and of excellent character. Tell me, will I marry her?"

"What is your name and address?" asked the old man.

Wei Ku told him. The old man leafed through the pages of the volume in his hand. Then he looked up and said, "I am afraid not. You see all marriages are written down in this book. I see here that your wife is only three years old now. But when she is seventeen, you will marry her. Do not worry."

"Do not worry!" exclaimed Wei. "You mean I shall have to remain a bachelor for another fourteen years?"

"That is the way it is."

"So I shall not be married to the daughter of the Pam family?"

"That is correct."

Wei did not know whether to believe him or not. Then he asked, "What have you got in that bag?"

"Silk strings. You see," said the old man, "this is all part of my job. I note the different pairs to be matched off in the book. When a baby girl and a baby boy are born and are fated to become man and wife, I go around in the night and tie their feet together. Once the knot is tied, nothing can separate them. After the strings are tied, they become invisible to everyone but me."

The old man smiled at Wei. "Yes," he said, "one may be born into a poor family, and the other wealthy. Or they may be separated by thousands of miles, or there may even be a **feud** between the two families. But they will end up as man and wife. There is nothing they can do about it."

"You have tied mine, I suppose," said Wei.

"Yes, I have."

"And where is the three-year-old baby who you say will one day be my wife?"

"Oh, she lives with a woman who sells vegetables at the market. It is not far from here. The woman comes to the market every day. If you are interested, follow me to the market after daybreak, and I will point her out to you."

Dawn had just broken, but the matchmaker who had made the appointment with Wei failed to arrive. "You see," remarked the old man, "there is no use waiting for him."

Wei decided to wait a while longer. They chatted together and Wei found the old man very pleasant to talk with. The old man told him that he liked his job immensely. "It is amazing," he said, "what a thin piece of string does. I see the boy and girl grow up, each in his or her home, sometimes unaware of the other's existence. But when the time comes, they meet and fall head over heels in love with each other. All they know is that they cannot help it. And if some other boy or girl comes in between, that person stumbles over the string or becomes tangled up in it and eventually gets discouraged. I have seen it happen again and again."

By now the market, which was only a short distance away, was filling up with people.

"Come, follow me," said the old man as he picked up his bag and arose.

When they came to the market, the old man pointed to a stall where a very dirty old woman with floppy, uncombed hair was selling vegetables. She seemed to be arguing shrilly with everyone in a loud, coarse voice. At her side was a skinny, ragged child.

"There she is," said the old man. "That child will be your wife."

"What do you mean?" said Wei. "You are joking with me." He turned angrily to the old man.

"No, I can assure you that child will marry you, live in comfort, and become a lady of high rank."

Wei looked at the thin, shabby child and was upset. He would have liked to dispute the old man's words, but when he turned around again the old man had vanished.

Wei went home disappointed because the matchmaker who was supposed to meet him had not arrived, and because he could not make up his mind whether or not to believe the old man. The more he thought about it, the more he found the idea of marrying that dirty child unpleasant, ridiculous, and **absurd**. He worried about it so much that he could not sleep that night.

In the morning Wei, greatly troubled, told his servant about what had happened the day before.

"There is no need to be concerned," said the servant. "After all, it is possible that the child will not live to the age of seventeen. Then there is no way you two could be married."

Later the servant went to the market. He found the woman in the stall, holding the baby. When the opportunity presented itself, the servant flashed out his knife, stabbed at the baby, and ran away. While the child cried loudly, the woman shouted "Murder!" and there was great confusion in the market. During this time the servant made his escape.

When he returned home, the servant revealed to Wei all that he had done.

"I see," said Wei, "so you killed the child?"

"No," replied the servant. "As I aimed the knife at her, the child turned suddenly. I think I only scraped her face near the eyebrow."

Wei was very distressed about what had happened. He hurriedly left the town and the incident was soon forgotten.

Wei then left for the capital, and disappointed that his match with the daughter of the Pam family had failed to come about, he turned his thoughts away from marriage. But three years later, a matchmaker arranged an excellent marriage with a young woman from the Tan family, a family well known in society. The woman was very well educated and famous for her beauty. Everyone congratulated Wei and preparations were made for the wedding. Then one morning he heard the terrible news that his proposed bride had run away and could not be found. It seems that she was in love with another man.

For two years, Wei stopped thinking about marriage. He was twenty-eight by now, and had given up the idea of marrying a woman from a well-known family. One day when he stopped at a temple in the countryside, he met the daughter of a farmer and eventually fell in love with her. Moreover, the woman was madly in love with him. They became engaged and he went to the capital to buy her silks and jewels. On his return he found that his fiancée had been struck by a serious disease. He was willing to wait but the illness dragged on, and after a year she had lost all her hair and had become blind. She decided not to marry Wei and insisted he find another woman to be his wife, for she refused to be a burden to him.

Several years passed before the perfect match was made. The woman was attractive and young, and was a great lover of books and music and art. There were no rivals and they became engaged. Three days before her wedding, when she was walking on a stone street, she tripped over a loose rock, fell down, hit her head, and died. It seemed as though fate was **mocking** Wei.

Wei Ku became completely discouraged and decided that he no longer wished to get married. He worked at the court in the city, carried out his responsibilities to the best of his ability, and thought no more about marrying. But he did his work so well that the chief judge suggested that his niece be married to Wei Ku.

The subject was painful to Wei. "Why do you want your niece to be married to me?" he asked. "I am getting too old to marry, and I always seem to bring bad luck to any woman who would marry me."

The judge persisted and Wei, under pressure, consented, but without enthusiasm. He did not see his bride until the wedding day, but she was young and very pleasant and he was pleased. She proved to be a good wife to Wei and they grew to love each other very dearly.

Wei thought that his wife was very attractive, but she always combed her hair in an unusual way over her right temple. Then one day Wei said to her, "Why don't you ever change the style of your hair? Why do you always let it fall to one side?"

She slowly lifted her hair and said, "This is why—to cover the scar from this wound which I received at the market when I was only three!"

SELECTING DETAILS FROM THE STORY.
Each of the following sentences helps
you understand the story. Complete each
sentence below by putting an *x* in the
box next to the correct answer.

1. The old man said that Wei Ku would
   - ☐ a. never get married.
   - ☐ b. marry a daughter of the Pam family.
   - ☐ c. marry someone who was only three years old now.

2. Wei's servant went to the market and attempted to
   - ☐ a. speak to the old woman.
   - ☐ b. find the old man.
   - ☐ c. kill the child.

3. Wei became engaged to a woman who
   - ☐ a. refused to marry him just hours before the wedding.
   - ☐ b. tripped on a rock, hit her head, and died.
   - ☐ c. admitted, at the last moment, that she already was married.

4. Finally, Wei married a woman who
   - ☐ a. combed her hair in an unusual way.
   - ☐ b. was several years older than he.
   - ☐ c. had visited him often at the court in the city.

HANDLING STORY ELEMENTS. Each of
the following questions reviews your
understanding of story elements. Put
an *x* in the box next to the correct
answer to each question.

1. Who is the *main character* in the "Matrimony Inn"?
   - ☐ a. Wei Ku
   - ☐ b. Wei Ku's servant
   - ☐ c. an old man from the spirit world

2. What happened first in the *plot* of the story?
   - ☐ a. Wei Ku's wife showed Wei a scar on her forehead.
   - ☐ b. Wei's servant went to the market to look for the child.
   - ☐ c. Wei came upon an old man who was reading a book by the light of the moon.

3. When is "Matrimony Inn" *set*?
   - ☐ a. at the present time
   - ☐ b. in the distant past
   - ☐ c. in the future

4. Which sentence best tells the *theme* of the story?
   - ☐ a. After she is struck by a serious disease, a woman decides not to marry.
   - ☐ b. A man never succeeds in finding a wife.
   - ☐ c. After many years have passed, the words of an old man come true.

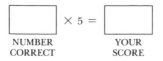

NUMBER
CORRECT   × 5 =   YOUR
SCORE

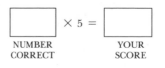

NUMBER
CORRECT   × 5 =   YOUR
SCORE

OBSERVING NEW VOCABULARY WORDS. Answer the following vocabulary questions by putting an *x* in the box next to the correct answer. The vocabulary words are printed in **boldface** in the story. If you wish, look back at the words before you answer the questions.

1. Since Wei Ku was a mortal, he could not understand the book from the spirit world. The word *mortal* means
   ☐ a. human being.
   ☐ b. ghost.
   ☐ c. fool.

2. Even a feud between their families could not keep them from marrying. What is the meaning of the word *feud*?
   ☐ a. a long, bitter quarrel
   ☐ b. a friendly discussion
   ☐ c. an angry letter

3. The idea that he would marry that ragged child was ridiculous and absurd to Wei. Something that is *absurd*
   ☐ a. makes sense.
   ☐ b. doesn't make sense.
   ☐ c. is expected.

4. Bad luck continually followed Wei; it seemed as though fate was mocking him. The word *mocking* means
   ☐ a. protecting.
   ☐ b. delaying.
   ☐ c. making fun of.

COMPLETING A CLOZE PASSAGE. Complete the following paragraph by filling in each blank with one of the words listed in the box below. Each of the words appears in the story. Since there are five words and four blanks, one word in the group will not be used.

Lin Yutang's best _____
                              1

story is probably "The Jade Goddess." It

_____ the story of Chang Po,
              2

a great artist who carves marvelous

figures out of jade. Chang Po

_____ a man by accident, is
              3

accused of murder, and is forced to flee.

The beautiful jade figures he continues

to make _____ lead his enemies
                        4

to him.

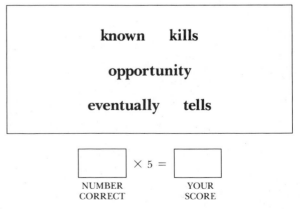

known   kills

opportunity

eventually   tells

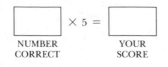

☐ × 5 = ☐
NUMBER   YOUR
CORRECT   SCORE

☐ × 5 = ☐
NUMBER   YOUR
CORRECT   SCORE

116

KNOWING HOW TO READ CRITICALLY. Each of the following questions will help you to think critically about the selection. Put an *x* in the box next to the correct answer.

1. We may infer that Wei's wife was
   - ☐ a. sorry that she married Wei.
   - ☐ b. about the same age as Wei.
   - ☐ c. the child who was stabbed by Wei's servant years ago.

2. It is reasonable to conclude that Wei got married
   - ☐ a. 10 years after he met the old man.
   - ☐ b. 14 years after he met the old man.
   - ☐ c. 20 years after he met the old man.

3. Wei probably decided that he no longer wished to get married because
   - ☐ a. he had had so many unhappy experiences earlier.
   - ☐ b. he was too busy to think about marriage.
   - ☐ c. the woman he loved had died in a fall.

4. The ending of the story showed that the old man
   - ☐ a. didn't have any special powers.
   - ☐ b. was only teasing Wei.
   - ☐ c. did arrange marriages.

Questions for Writing and Discussion

- No matter what Wei's servant did, he would not have been able to kill the child. Do you agree or disagree with this statement? Explain your answer.
- Why did Wei complain, "I always seem to bring bad luck to any woman who would marry me"? Give examples in your answer.
- After Wei's wife showed Wei the scar on her forehead, do you think he told her how she received it? Why? What would you have said if you were Wei?

Use the boxes below to total your scores for the exercises. Then write your score on pages 150 and 151.

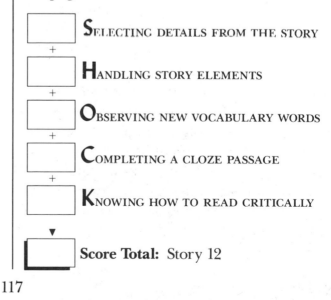

☐
  \+
SELECTING DETAILS FROM THE STORY

☐
  \+
HANDLING STORY ELEMENTS

☐
  \+
OBSERVING NEW VOCABULARY WORDS

☐
  \+
COMPLETING A CLOZE PASSAGE

☐
▼
KNOWING HOW TO READ CRITICALLY

☐ **Score Total:** Story 12

☐ × 5 = ☐

NUMBER   YOUR
CORRECT   SCORE

13

Rain, Rain, Go Away

by Isaac Asimov

*T*here she is again," said Lillian Wright as she adjusted the blinds carefully. "There she is, George."

"There who is?" asked her husband, settling down in front of the TV to watch the ball game.

"Mrs. Sakkaro," she said. "The new neighbors, that's who."

"Oh."

"Sunbathing. Always sunbathing in the yard. I wonder where her boy is. He's usually outside on a nice day like this, standing in that tremendous yard of theirs, throwing the ball against the house. Did you ever see him, George?"

"I've *heard* him. It's torture. Bang on the wall, smack in the hand. Bang, smack, bang—"

"He's a nice boy, quiet and well-behaved. I wish Tommie would make friends with him. He's Tommie's age, too, just about ten, I should say."

"I didn't know Tommie was shy about making friends."

"Well, it's hard with the Sakkaros. They keep to themselves so much. I don't even know what Mr. Sakkaro does."

"Why should you? It's not really anyone's business what he does."

"It's odd that I never see him go to work."

"No one ever sees me go to work."

"You stay at home and write. What does *he* do?"

"Well, Mrs. Sakkaro knows what Mr. Sakkaro does and is probably all upset because she doesn't know what *I* do."

"Oh, George." Lillian retreated from the window. "I think we should make an effort."

"What kind of an effort?" George was comfortable on the couch now, with a soda, freshly opened and cold, in his hand.

"To get to know them."

"Well, didn't you make an effort when she first moved in? You said you called."

"I said hello. But, well, she'd just moved in and the house was still upset, so that it was just hello. It's been two months now and it's still nothing more than hello, occasionally. She's so odd."

"Is she?"

"She's always looking at the sky. I've seen her do it a hundred times. And she's never been out when it's the least bit cloudy. Once, when her boy was out playing, she called to him to come in, shouting that it was going to rain. I happened to hear her and looked up and, you know, it was broad daylight. Oh, there were some clouds, but nothing really."

"Did it rain eventually?"

"Of course not."

George called out to Lillian, who was vanishing into the kitchen. "Well, since they're from Arizona where it doesn't rain that much, they probably don't know rain clouds from other clouds."

Lillian came back into the living room. "From where?"

"From Arizona, according to Tommie."

"How did Tommie know?"

"He talked to their boy, in the yard, I guess, and he told Tommie they came from Arizona. And then the boy was called inside. At least, Tommie says it might have been Arizona, or maybe Alabama or some place like that. But if they're that nervous about the weather, I guess it's Arizona and they don't know what to make of a good rainy climate like ours."

"But why didn't you ever tell me?"

"Because Tommie only told me this morning and because I thought he must have told you already. Wow—"

The ball went sailing out over the fence.

Lillian went back to the blinds and said, "I'll simply just have to make her acquaintance. She looks very nice. Oh, look at that, George."

George was looking at nothing but the TV.

Lillian said, "She's staring at that cloud. And now she's going inside. Honestly."

Two days later George had just come back from the library with some books. Lillian, with a big smile on her face, greeted him **jubilantly**.

She said, "Now, you're not doing anything tomorrow."

"That sounds like a statement, not a question."

"It *is* a statement. We're going out with the Sakkaros to the carnival at Murphy's Park."

"With—"

"With the Sakkaros—our next-door neighbors."

"How did you arrange it?"

"I just went up to their house this morning and rang the bell. She was as sweet as could be. Invited me in, knew who I was, said she was so glad I had come to visit."

"And you suggested we go to Murphy's Park."

"Yes. I thought that if I suggested something that would let the children have fun, it would be easier for her to go along with it."

"I see."

"But you should see her home."

"Aha. You had a reason for all this. Now it comes out. You wanted to see her home. But, please, spare me the details. I'm not interested in the size of her closets."

"*Clean*," said Lillian. "I have never seen any place so spotless. Her kitchen was so clean you just couldn't believe that she ever used it. I asked for a drink of water and she held the glass underneath the faucet and poured slowly, so slowly that not one drop fell in the sink itself. She did it so casually that I just knew she *always* did it that way. And when she gave me the glass she held it—with a clean napkin!"

"She must give herself a lot of trouble," said George. "Did she agree to go with us right away?"

"Well—not right off. She called upstairs to her husband to find out what the weather forecast was. And he said that the newspapers all said it would be fair tomorrow, but that he was waiting for the latest report on the radio."

"*All* the newspapers said so, eh?"

"Of course they all print pretty much the same weather forecast, so they would all be about the same. But I think they do subscribe to several newspapers."

"There isn't much you miss, is there?" said George, smiling.

"Anyway," said Lillian, ignoring him, "she called up the weather bureau and had them give her the latest information and she called it out to her husband. And they said they'd go, except they said they'd phone us if there were any unexpected changes in the weather."

"All right. Then we'll go."

The Sakkaros were young and pleasant, dark and handsome. As they came down the long walk from their house to where the Wright automobile was parked, Lillian whispered, "What's that he's carrying?"

"Transistor radio. To listen to the weather forecast, I bet."

The Sakkaro boy came running after them, waving something which turned out to be a barometer.[1] All three got into the backseat of the car. Conversation, on not very personal subjects, lasted until they got to Murphy's Park.

---

1. **barometer:** an instrument that measures air pressure. It is used to forecast changes in the weather.

The Sakkaro boy was so polite and soft-spoken that even Tommie Wright, who was **wedged** between his parents in the front seat, followed his example. Lillian couldn't remember when she had spent so **serene** and peaceful a drive.

She was not at all bothered by the fact that, barely heard under the conversation, was the sound of Mr. Sakkaro's small radio. Occasionally he put it up to his ear.

It was a beautiful day at Murphy's Park. It was hot and dry without being too hot. And there was a cheerfully bright sun in a blue, blue sky. Even Mr. Sakkaro, though he inspected the sky with a careful eye and then stared closely at the barometer, seemed to find no fault.

Lillian went with the boys to the amusement section and bought each boy a ticket for every ride in the park.

"Please," she said to Mrs. Sakkaro who protested, "let this be my treat. It can be your treat the next time."

When she returned, George was alone. "Where are the Sakkaros?" she asked.

"Just down there at the refreshment stand. I told them I'd wait here for you and then we would join them. I think the Sakkaros must be independently wealthy," he added.

"Why?"

"I don't know if he does *anything* for a living. I kind of asked him and he said he's just a student of human nature."

"How interesting. That would explain why they have all those newspapers."

"And he doesn't come from Arizona."

"He doesn't?"

"I said I heard he was from Arizona. He looked so surprised that it was obvious he wasn't. Then he laughed and asked if he had an Arizona accent."

Lillian said thoughtfully, "But he does have some kind of accent, you know. It's hard to tell what it is. Come on, they're waving at us now. Oh, look what they've bought."

The Sakkaros were each holding three sticks of cotton candy—huge swirls of pink foam made of syrupy sugar that had been spun dry. It melted sweetly in the mouth and left one feeling sticky.

The Sakkaros held one stick of cotton candy out to Mr. and Mrs. Wright. Out of politeness, they accepted.

Then they tried their hand at darts, at games where balls were rolled into holes, at knocking down wooden dolls. They took pictures of themselves and tested their strength.

Eventually, they collected the youngsters and the Sakkaros went off with the boys instantly to the refreshment stand.

"Frankly," said George, "I prefer to stay here. If I see them biting away at another stick of cotton candy I'll turn green on the spot. If they haven't had a dozen each, I'll eat a dozen myself."

"I know, and they're buying a handful for their child now."

"I offered to buy Mr. Sakkaro a hamburger," said George, "and he just looked grim and shook his head."

"I know. I offered her an orange drink and the way she jumped when she said no, you'd have thought I threw it in her face. Still, I suppose they've never been to a place like this before, and they'll need time to adjust to the **novelty**. They'll fill up on cotton candy and then never eat it again for ten years."

"Well, maybe." They strolled toward the Sakkaros. "You know, Lillian," said George, "it's clouding up."

Mr. Sakkaro had the radio to his ears and was looking anxiously toward the west.

"Uh-oh," said George, "he's seen the clouds. Bet you anything he'll want to go home."

All three Sakkaros were upon him instantly, polite but insistent. They were sorry, they had had a wonderful time, a marvelous time, the Wrights would have to be their guests as soon as it could be arranged, but now, really, they had to go home. It looked stormy. Mrs. Sakkaro complained that all the weather forecasts had been for fair weather.

George tried to make them feel better. "It's hard to predict a local storm," he said. "But even if it were to come, and it might not, it surely wouldn't last for more than half an hour."

At this comment, the Sakkaro youngster seemed on the verge of tears. Mrs. Sakkaro's hand, holding a handkerchief, trembled visibly.

"Let's go home," said George, without discussing it further.

The drive back seemed to stretch on forever. There was hardly any conversation. Mr. Sakkaro's radio was quite loud now as he switched from station to station, picking up a weather report every time. They were mentioning "local thundershowers" now.

The Sakkaro youngster announced that the barometer was falling. Mrs. Sakkaro, her chin in the palm of her hand, stared unhappily at the sky and asked George if he could drive faster, please.

A wind had sprung up when they came to the street on which they lived. The leaves rustled and lightning flashed.

George said, "You'll be indoors in two minutes, friends. We'll make it."

He pulled up at the gate that opened onto the Sakkaro's large front yard and got out of the car to open the back door. He thought he felt a drop. They were *just* in time.

The Sakkaros tumbled out. Their faces were tense as they muttered thanks. Then they started running as fast as they could down their long front walk.

"Honestly," Lillian started to say, *"you would think they were—"*

The heavens opened and the rain came down in giant drops. The Sakkaros stopped and looked upward in despair. As the rain hit, their faces blurred and shrank and ran together. All three Sakkaros shriveled up and collapsed within their clothes, which sank down into three sticky heaps.

And while the Wrights sat there in horror, Lillian slowly completed her remark, *"—made of sugar and afraid they would melt."*

SELECTING DETAILS FROM THE STORY.
Each of the following sentences helps
you understand the story. Complete each
sentence below by putting an *x* in the
box next to the correct answer.

1. Lillian thought that Mrs. Sakkaro was
   odd because the new neighbor
   ☒ a. was always looking at the sky.
   ☐ b. came from another state.
   ☐ c. was always so cheerful.

2. When the Sakkaros went to Murphy's
   Park, they brought along
   ☐ a. enough food for everyone.
   ☐ b. some games for the boys.
   ☒ c. a small radio and a barometer.

3. As soon as the weather changed at the
   park, the Sakkaros
   ☐ a. hurried to the refreshment stand
   to get cotton candy before
   leaving.
   ☒ b. announced that they had to go
   home.
   ☐ c. rushed inside to wait for the
   storm to pass.

4. At the end of the story, the Sakkaros
   ☐ a. walked slowly down their front
   walk.
   ☐ b. made it safely to their house.
   ☒ c. turned into three sticky heaps.

HANDLING STORY ELEMENTS. Each of
the following questions reviews your
understanding of story elements. Put
an *x* in the box next to the correct
answer to each question.

1. What happened last in the *plot* of
   "Rain, Rain, Go Away"?
   ☐ a. Lillian said they should make
   an effort to get to know the
   Sakkaros better.
   ☒ b. The Sakkaros ran as fast as they
   could down their long front walk.
   ☐ c. Lillian bought each boy a ticket
   for the rides.

2. Which sentence best *characterizes*
   the Sakkaros?
   ☐ a. They were very friendly.
   ☐ b. They hated the sun.
   ☒ c. They were terrified of water.

3. The ending of the story is *set*
   ☒ a. on the street where the Wrights
   and the Sakkaros lived.
   ☐ b. at a refreshment stand in a park.
   ☐ c. somewhere in Arizona.

4. Which sentence best tells the *theme* of
   the story?
   ☐ a. Whenever possible, one should
   try to make friends with new
   neighbors.
   ☐ b. You can have a very enjoyable
   time at a carnival.
   ☒ c. New neighbors are destroyed when
   rain exposes their amazing secret.

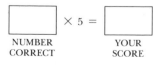

NUMBER   YOUR
CORRECT   SCORE

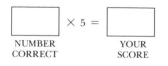

NUMBER   YOUR
CORRECT   SCORE

125

OBSERVING NEW VOCABULARY WORDS. Answer the following vocabulary questions by putting an *x* in the box next to the correct answer. The vocabulary words are printed in **boldface** in the story. If you wish, look back at the words before you answer the questions.

1. With a big smile on her face, Lillian greeted her husband jubilantly. What is the meaning of the word *jubilantly*?
   - ☐ a. angrily
   - ☒ b. joyfully
   - ☐ c. suspiciously

2. Tommy Wright was wedged between his parents in the front seat of the car. The word *wedged* means
   - ☐ a. lost.
   - ☐ b. thrown.
   - ☒ c. squeezed.

3. Because the boys were so polite and quiet, the drive to the park was serene and peaceful. The word *serene* means
   - ☒ a. calm.
   - ☐ b. amazing.
   - ☐ c. noisy.

4. Lillian said that the Sakkaros probably had "never been to a place like this before, and they'll need time to adjust to the novelty." As used here, the word *novelty* means
   - ☐ a. a gift.
   - ☐ b. bright sunshine.
   - ☒ c. a new thing.

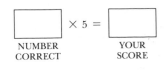

NUMBER CORRECT × 5 = YOUR SCORE

COMPLETING A CLOZE PASSAGE. Complete the following paragraph by filling in each blank with one of the words listed in the box below. Each of the words appears in the story. Since there are five words and four blanks, one word in the group will not be used.

The next time you complain about the _____ , think about the following facts. In Cherrapunji, India, it _____ 1,041 inches in one year. That is the record for the heaviest rainfall during any twelve _____ . In Iquique, Chile, on the _____ hand, it did not rain for fourteen years.

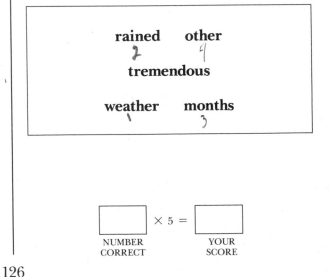

rained
2
other
4

tremendous

weather
1
months
3

NUMBER CORRECT × 5 = YOUR SCORE

126

KNOWING HOW TO READ CRITICALLY. Each of the following questions will help you to think critically about the selection. Put an *x* in the box next to the correct answer.

1. What happened to the Sakkaros at the end of the story?
   - ☐ a. They decided to move to another neighborhood.
   - ☐ b. They arrived home exhausted but happy.
   - ☒ c. They melted in the rain.

2. Evidence in the story indicates that the Sakkaros were
   - ☐ a. a wealthy family from Arizona.
   - ☐ b. ordinary people who were somewhat shy.
   - ☒ c. aliens, or creatures from another planet.

3. We may infer that the Sakkaros loved to eat cotton candy because
   - ☒ a. they were made of sugar.
   - ☐ b. cotton candy contains many vitamins and minerals.
   - ☐ c. they liked to eat or drink anything sweet.

4. Why were the Sakkaros so concerned about changes in the weather?
   - ☐ a. They were afraid they might catch a cold.
   - ☐ b. They hadn't brought any warm clothing with them.
   - ☒ c. They had to avoid rain because it would destroy them.

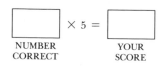

NUMBER CORRECT   × 5 =   YOUR SCORE

Questions for Writing and Discussion

- When George asked him if he came from Arizona, Mr. Sakkaro looked surprised and laughed. Why do you think Mr. Sakkaro acted that way? Where do you think the Sakkaros came from?
- When she gave Lillian a glass of water, Mrs. Sakkaro held it with a clean napkin. Why? Why did Mrs. Sakkaro jump when Lillian offered her an orange drink?
- According to Lillian, Mrs. Sakkaro "was as sweet as could be." What is amusing about that remark? Why is this story called, "Rain, Rain, Go Away"? Think of another title that would also be fitting.

Use the boxes below to total your scores for the exercises. Then write your score on pages 150 and 151.

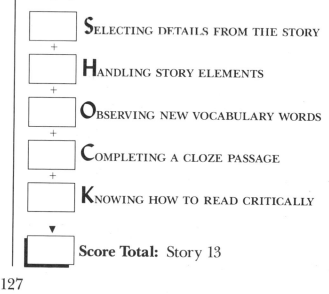

SELECTING DETAILS FROM THE STORY

+

HANDLING STORY ELEMENTS

+

OBSERVING NEW VOCABULARY WORDS

+

COMPLETING A CLOZE PASSAGE

+

KNOWING HOW TO READ CRITICALLY

▼

Score Total: Story 13

14

The Wind in the Rosebush

by Mary E. Wilkins Freeman

The ferry was waiting when Rebecca Flint got off the train with her suitcase. Minutes later she was safely on board, and heading toward Ford's Village on the other side of the river.

Next to Rebecca sat a woman of about her own age who kept sneaking curious glances at her. The woman's husband stood near her. Rebecca paid no attention to either of them. Rebecca herself was tall and thin, with gray hair, and a frown which seemed to have settled permanently on her face.

"It's a pleasant day, today," the other woman finally said to Rebecca.

"Yes, very," Rebecca agreed.

"Have you come from very far?" the woman asked.

"All the way from Michigan," Rebecca replied. She paused, then asked, "Do you know John Dent's widow who lives in Ford's Village? John Dent died about three years ago."

The woman jumped violently and turned pale. Then she cast a strange glance at her husband. He was shaking his head and giving her a look of warning.

"Yes, I guess I do," the woman finally remarked.

"His first wife was my sister," said Rebecca.

"Was she?" the other woman said nervously.

"I'm on my way to see Mrs. Dent now. I plan to take my niece Agnes home with me," Rebecca added.

At this, the woman was so startled that Rebecca quickly asked, "What's the matter? Is my niece sick?"

"No, she's not sick," replied the woman hastily. Then she caught her breath with a gasp.

"When did you see her?"

"Let me think. I haven't seen her for some time now."

"What kind of woman is the second wife?"

"I—guess Mrs. Dent's a nice woman," was the reply. "I— don't know. I—don't see much of her."

"When John Dent died," said Rebecca, "I couldn't help much with my niece, Agnes. My own mother was ill at the time and I had to take care of her. But now she's passed away and left me quite a bit of money, so I've come for the girl. I guess she'll be glad enough to go with me. I understand that her stepmother has always considered her something of a burden. I suppose, though, she's always taken care of her well enough."

The man gave his wife another sharp, warning look.

"I guess so," she said softly.

At that moment the ferry pulled up to the shore. Mrs. Dent had sent a driver to meet her sister-in-law. As Rebecca went off with him, the woman turned to her husband and said, frowning, "It seems to me I should have told her, Thomas."

"Let her find it out herself," replied the man. "There's no point in burning your fingers in other people's pudding."

The driver stopped in front of a small, white cottage. Moments later, a large woman with light hair and suspicious blue eyes, extended her hand to Rebecca. "You are Miss Flint, I suppose," she said in a cautious and wary manner.

"Yes," replied Rebecca, noticing, with surprise, a combination of fear and defiance on Mrs. Dent's face.

"Your letter arrived just this morning," Mrs. Dent said in a very cool voice.

"Yes," replied Rebecca. "From what John used to write, I thought you could probably put me up for a little while without it causing too much trouble. When I inherited that money, I was eager to come as quickly as possible for Agnes. I believed from what I heard that you would be willing to give her up. John always said she looked just like my sister."

Rebecca suddenly stopped and stared at the other woman in amazement and alarm. Mrs. Dent was standing there speechless, gasping, her lips parted in a strange and frightening way.

"Are you sick?" exclaimed Rebecca. "Do you want me to get you some water?"

Mrs. Dent recovered with a great effort. "No," she said, breathing deeply, "it is nothing. I am subject to—spells. But I am over it now. Won't you come in, Miss Flint?"

As they entered the house Rebecca noticed, on the open porch, a rose-bush which had been planted in a pot. And though it was very late in the season, one small red rose was growing on the bush. Suddenly, Mrs. Dent shook a warning hand at Rebecca. "Don't you pick that rose!" she cried abruptly.

Rebecca drew herself up with stiff **dignity**. "I am not in the habit of picking other people's flowers," she responded.

But even as Rebecca spoke, she was startled by something extremely strange that happened. The rosebush began to suddenly shake wildly, as though being blown by gusts of wind. Yet the day was calm and the air was still.

"What on earth—" began Rebecca. "How can that rosebush shake when there isn't any breeze?"

"I don't see that it is shaking," answered the other woman, calmly. And as she spoke, the bush, indeed, was still.

"I tell you it was moving!" Rebecca persisted.

"It isn't now," said Mrs. Dent. "I can't account for everything you think you see. I have too many things to do."

"Strange," remarked Rebecca, uneasily, as she followed Mrs. Dent into the house.

When the two women were seated at tea, Rebecca told Mrs. Dent, "It's certainly pleasant here." Then she glanced out the window and asked, "Shouldn't Agnes be coming home soon?"

"Pretty soon," answered Mrs. Dent. "But when she goes over to Addie Slocum's house, she loses track of the time and never seems to know when to leave."

"Is Addie Slocum her best friend?"

"As close as any," said Mrs. Dent.

Just then Rebecca looked up suddenly, for she noticed someone passing by outside the window.

"There she is!" Rebecca said in an excited voice.

"She isn't as late as I thought she'd be," said Mrs. Dent. And a strange expression passed over her face.

For several moments Rebecca stared at the door, waiting for it to open. "Where *is* Agnes?" she asked, finally. "Why doesn't she come in?"

By way of answer, Mrs. Dent got up stiffly, walked across the room, and threw open the door.

"Agnes!" she called. "Agnes!" Then she turned and looked back at Rebecca. "She's not here."

"But I saw her pass by the window," said Rebecca, bewildered.

"You must have been mistaken."

"I know I saw her," Rebecca insisted.

"You couldn't have!"

"But I did—"

"What did she look like?" asked Mrs. Dent.

"Small with light hair—her hair was tossed to one side of her forehead."

"You couldn't have seen her."

"Does Agnes look like that?"

"A little like that," said Mrs. Dent. "But *of course* you didn't see her. You've been thinking about her so much that you *thought* you did. It's too early for her to come home from Addie Slocum's."

When Rebecca went to bed that evening, Agnes had not yet returned. At first, Rebecca promised herself that she would stay up until her niece came home. But she was tired from the trip, and decided that she would wait until the following day to see her.

At breakfast the next morning, Rebecca asked Mrs. Dent, "What time did Agnes get home last night?"

"She didn't get home."

"What?"

"She didn't come home. She stayed overnight at Addie's house. She often does."

"Without sending you word?"

"Oh, she knew I wouldn't worry."

"When will she be home?"

"Pretty soon, I guess."

Rebecca waited as patiently as she could, but at four o'clock she approached Mrs. Dent. "I've been waiting here ever since yesterday—twenty-four hours," she said, "and I still haven't seen Agnes. I came all the way from Michigan to see her. I want you to send for her."

Mrs. Dent considered this for a moment, then said, "Well I don't blame you. It's high time she came home. I'll go right over and get her myself."

Rebecca breathed a sigh of relief as Mrs. Dent went out.

For a long time Rebecca sat staring out the window. Finally she saw Mrs. Dent coming up the path. She was walking alone. Rebecca ran to the door. As she did, she noticed that the rosebush was again shaking wildly—though there wasn't the slightest breeze in the room!

"Where is Agnes?" asked Rebecca urgently.

Mrs. Dent forced a smile as she said slowly, "She's gone with Addie to visit Addie's aunt in Lincoln. She'll be there for a few days. Mrs. Slocum said Agnes didn't have time to come back and ask me before the train left. But she took it upon herself to say it was all right."

"How far is Lincoln from here?" asked Rebecca.

"About fifty miles."

"That will keep me here longer than I planned," said Rebecca.

"If you don't feel you can wait, please don't stay," Mrs. Dent said sweetly. "I'll get Agnes ready and send her on *later*—as soon as I can."

Rebecca glared at Mrs. Dent. "It seems I'll just have to wait after all," she said grimly.

That night Rebecca was awakened from a deep sleep a little after midnight. She lay in bed for a minute listening to a melody. It was coming from the piano in the living room below. She could hear it quite clearly—"The Dance of Spring." Rebecca jumped up and, trembling, hurried down the stairs. She rushed into the room. No one was there. The piano was silent.

Confused and upset, Rebecca made her way to Mrs. Dent's bedroom and banged on the door.

A moment later, Mrs. Dent stood before Rebecca, staring at her stonily.

"Who—who was that playing on the piano?" demanded Rebecca.

"I didn't hear anybody."

"There was somebody playing."

"I didn't hear anything."

"I tell you there was someone. *But there isn't anyone there!* Has Agnes come home? *I want to know.*"

"Of course Agnes hasn't come home!"

"I heard somebody—playing on the piano."

"You were dreaming."

Rebecca shook her head. "I wasn't," she said sharply. "I was wide awake!"

Rebecca turned and went back to her room where all night long she lay in bed, thinking. The next morning she came downstairs and said to Mrs. Dent, "I want to know where the Slocums live."

Mrs. Dent gave her a long, strange look. "Why?" she asked, finally.

"Tell me," said Rebecca, "does Agnes play the piano?"

"She plays it a little."

"Does she ever play 'The Dance of Spring'?"

Mrs. Dent paused. "That's her favorite song."

Rebecca's face looked solemn. "I'm worried about what happened last night. I want to ask the Slocums if they've heard anything about their daughter or Agnes."

"You're being absurd," said Mrs. Dent, as she **reluctantly** gave Rebecca the directions.

About two hours later Rebecca returned. Her face was red and showed **distress**. "I went there," she said, "and there isn't anyone home. Something *has* happened."

"That doesn't mean much of anything," said Mrs. Dent, coolly. "Mr. Slocum is a conductor on the railroad here. He's frequently away. When he's gone, Mrs. Slocum often leaves early to spend the day with her sister."

"Then you don't think anything has happened?" asked Rebecca, doubtfully.

"Certainly not."

Confused, Rebecca went upstairs to hang up her coat. But she rushed back down with the coat still on. "Someone's been in my room!" she gasped. Her face was pale.

"Why, what do you mean?" Mrs. Dent asked slowly.

"When I went upstairs, I found on the bed—that little red rose!"

Mrs. Dent stared at Rebecca with eyes full of anger. "What do you mean by talking such nonsense?" she demanded.

I tell you the rose is on the bed.

"Look at that bush," Mrs. Dent replied.

Rebecca hurried from the room. When she came back, her eyes were open wide. "The rose is gone from the bed. Now it's back on the bush! What's going on around here?"

"Nothing's going on here. Are you crazy or something?"

"No, I'm not crazy yet," said Rebecca. "But I will be if this goes on much longer. I'm going to find out where Agnes is tonight. I'm going to Lincoln."

However Rebecca did not go. A violent blinding rain came up, which made travel impossible. Then in the evening a letter arrived from the Michigan village that Rebecca had left.

Rebecca had asked a friend to stay at the house while she was gone. The letter informed Rebecca that the friend had fallen down the cellar stairs and broken her hip. It was necessary for Rebecca to return at once.

Rebecca looked at Mrs. Dent who had given her the letter. "Where did this come from?" she asked.

"Mr. Amblecrom brought it," was the reply.

"Who's he?"

"The postmaster. He often delivers the letters that arrive late in the day. He said that he and his wife came over on the ferry with you."

"I remember him," Rebecca replied. "There's bad news in this letter."

"Really?"

"Yes. My friend has fallen down the cellar stairs—they were always dangerous—and she's broken her hip. I've got to take the first train home tomorrow."

"You don't say so. I'm terribly sorry."

"No, you're not sorry," Rebecca said, pointedly. "You're glad. I don't know why, but you're glad. For some reason you've wanted to get rid of me ever since I came. I don't know why. You're a strange person, Mrs. Dent. Now you've got your way, and I hope you're satisfied."

"You're talking nonsense," said Mrs. Dent in a voice that suggested she was hurt. But Rebecca noticed the slight smile that crossed her face.

"Well, I'm going tomorrow morning. As soon as Agnes gets home send her to me. Pack whatever clothes and things she's got and buy her a ticket. I'll leave the money, and you can send her along. She doesn't have to change cars, just see her to the train."

"Very well," said Mrs. Dent, still looking amused.

Rebecca started on her journey the next morning. When she arrived home, she found her friend in perfect health. There was no clue as to who had written the letter.

Rebecca would have returned to Ford's Village the following day. However, she woke up with a fever and felt too ill to travel. But she could write, and she did, to the Slocums, and she received no answer. She also wrote to Mrs. Dent. She even sent several telegrams and got no **response**. Finally she wrote a letter to the postmaster. She received a prompt answer.

The letter was short and to the point. Mr. Amblecrom, the postmaster, was a man of few words. He wrote

Dear Madam,

Received your letter. No Slocums in Ford's Village. All dead. Addie died ten years ago. Her mother and father killed five years later in an accident. House vacant. Mrs. John Dent said to have neglected stepdaughter. Girl was sick. Medicine not given. There was talk of the town taking action. Not enough evidence. House said to be haunted. Strange sights and sounds there. Your niece, Agnes Dent, died a year ago, about this time.

Yours truly,
Thomas Amblecrom

SELECTING DETAILS FROM THE STORY.
Each of the following sentences helps
you understand the story. Complete each
sentence below by putting an *x* in the
box next to the correct answer.

1. When Rebecca said she had come to
   get Agnes, Mrs. Dent
   ☐ a. smiled and thanked Rebecca.
   ☐ b. ordered Rebecca out of the house.
   ☐ c. stood speechless and looked ill.

2. One night, a little after midnight,
   Rebecca was awakened by
   ☐ a. the sound of Agnes tapping at
         the window.
   ☐ b. a loud train whistle.
   ☐ c. piano music.

3. When Rebecca went to her room after
   returning from the Slocum's, she was
   shocked to find a
   ☐ a. red rose on the bed.
   ☐ b. warning note from Mrs. Dent.
   ☐ c. picture of Agnes that someone
         had slipped under the door.

4. The letter from Thomas Amblecrom
   stated that Mrs. Dent
   ☐ a. was a wonderful mother.
   ☐ b. neglected her stepdaughter.
   ☐ c. had just moved away.

HANDLING STORY ELEMENTS. Each of
the following questions reviews your
understanding of story elements. Put
an *x* in the box next to the correct
answer to each question.

1. "The Wind in the Rosebush" is *set* in
   ☐ a. Ford's Village.
   ☐ b. a city in Michigan.
   ☐ c. a town named Lincoln.

2. What happened last in the *plot* of
   the story?
   ☐ a. Rebecca heard a melody coming
         from the living room.
   ☐ b. Mrs. Dent said she would go to
         the Slocum's to get Agnes.
   ☐ c. Rebecca received a letter from
         Mr. Amblecrom.

3. Because of the author's *style* of writing,
   "The Wind in the Rosebush" may be
   described as a
   ☐ a. love story.
   ☐ b. story of space travel.
   ☐ c. kind of ghost story.

4. Which of the following best tells the
   theme of the story?
   ☐ a. A woman is forced to return home
         early when a friend is injured.
   ☐ b. When an aunt attempts to bring
         home her neice, she has a series
         of strange experiences.
   ☐ c. A rosebush shakes wildly,
         although there isn't any breeze
         at the time.

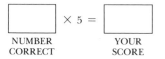

NUMBER   YOUR
CORRECT   SCORE

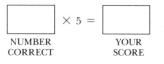

NUMBER   YOUR
CORRECT   SCORE

OBSERVING NEW VOCABULARY WORDS.
Answer the following vocabulary questions by putting an *x* in the box next to the correct answer. The vocabulary words are printed in **boldface** in the story. If you wish, look back at the words before you answer the questions.

1. When Rebecca discovered that there was no one at the Slocums' house, her face became red and showed distress. As used here, the word *distress* means
   ☐ a. relief.
   ☐ b. imagination.
   ☐ c. grief.

2. Mrs. Dent reluctantly gave Rebecca the Slocums' address. The word *reluctantly* means
   ☐ a. slowly and hesitantly.
   ☐ b. willingly and readily.
   ☐ c. gladly and happily.

3. Rebecca sent several telegrams but got no response. What is the meaning of the word *response*?
   ☐ a. treasure
   ☐ b. answer
   ☐ c. welcome

4. When Mrs. Dent warned her about picking the rose, Rebecca drew herself up with stiff dignity. When you act with *dignity* you
   ☐ a. blame another person.
   ☐ b. challenge someone to a fight.
   ☐ c. show pride and self-respect.

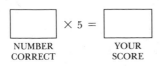

NUMBER
CORRECT   × 5 =   YOUR
SCORE

COMPLETING A CLOZE PASSAGE. Complete the following paragraph by filling in each blank with one of the words listed in the box below. Each of the words appears in the story. Since there are five words and four blanks, one word in the group will not be used.

No _____ has been
1

celebrated more in literature and art

than the rose. For example, more poems

have been _____ about the rose
2

than any other flower. Why the rose has

captured the imagination so, no one can

say for _____. Still, no one
3

_____ that the rose is the most
4

popular flower.

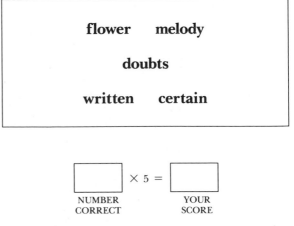

flower   melody

doubts

written   certain

NUMBER
CORRECT   × 5 =   YOUR
SCORE

KNOWING HOW TO READ CRITICALLY. Each of the following questions will help you to think critically about the selection. Put an *x* in the box next to the correct answer.

1. Which statement is true?
   - ☐ a. It was not possible for Agnes to return with Rebecca because Agnes had died.
   - ☐ b. Mrs. Dent was pleased that Rebecca was willing to take care of Agnes.
   - ☐ c. Agnes was spending a few days with Addie Slocum's aunt.

2. Mr. Amblecrom told his wife, "There's no point in burning your fingers in other people's pudding." That means
   - ☐ a. you should be willing to help a person in need.
   - ☐ b. you should stay out of other people's business.
   - ☐ c. good manners at the dinner table are important.

3. Clues in the story suggest that
   - ☐ a. Mrs. Dent was a kind person.
   - ☐ b. the ghost of Agnes sometimes appeared at the house.
   - ☐ c. Rebecca enjoyed her visit with Mrs. Dent.

4. Mr. Amblecrom's letter suggests that Rebecca
   - ☐ a. had a very lively imagination.
   - ☐ b. was probably going crazy.
   - ☐ c. had stayed at a haunted house.

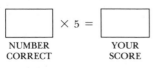

☐ × 5 = ☐

NUMBER CORRECT   YOUR SCORE

Questions for Writing and Discussion

- At least six very strange events occurred in "The Wind in the Rosebush." List as many of these as you can. Think of a reasonable explanation for one. (Do not suggest ghosts or things ghostly.)
- Why was Rebecca convinced that she had seen Agnes pass by the window? Why was Mrs. Dent certain that Rebecca was mistaken?
- Suppose that Mrs. Dent has received Rebecca's letter two weeks earlier. What do you think Mrs. Dent would have done? (Don't hesitate to use your imagination.)

Use the boxes below to total your scores for the exercises. Then write your score on pages 150 and 151.

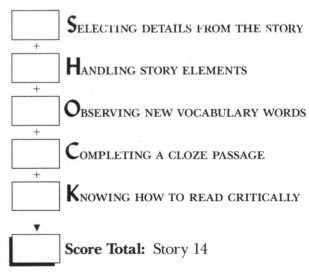

☐ **S**ELECTING DETAILS FROM THE STORY

+

☐ **H**ANDLING STORY ELEMENTS

+

☐ **O**BSERVING NEW VOCABULARY WORDS

+

☐ **C**OMPLETING A CLOZE PASSAGE

+

☐ **K**NOWING HOW TO READ CRITICALLY

▼

☐ **Score Total:** Story 14

15

The Donkey Goes to Market

by Alice Geer Kelsey

I tell you, no! I will not keep this miserable donkey another day!" Nasr-ed-Din Hodja glared at the little gray donkey that was patiently switching off the myriad[1] flies as it waited for the Hodja to fasten on the piece of old rug that served as a saddle.

"A new donkey might be just as stubborn," suggested Fatima.

"This wretch is more than stubborn!" stormed the Hodja. "It eats like an elephant but grows skinnier every day. It is as slow as a tortoise, lazy as a pig, mean as a fox, stupid as a fish, and as stubborn as a—as a—as a donkey!"

Fatima patted the little donkey which rubbed its head **affectionately** against her striped sleeve. Fatima said nothing. She had argued with her husband enough times to know that it was like throwing dry leaves on a fire.

"Say your good-byes to the creature!" Nasr-ed-Din Hodja threw one long leg over the little animal. He made the low throaty "Ughr-r-r," which is marching orders to a Turkish donkey. "Next time you see it, someone else will be riding it. You shall see what a fine donkey I shall ride home from the animal market. You know how good I am at buying and selling. I can sell this wretched donkey for enough to buy a fine one, and still have a gold piece left over for you to sew in your headdress."

"Ughr-r-r," he whirred to the donkey again. The little animal reluctantly shook its long ears, picked up one tiny hoof, and was off. Gloating over the great bargain he was to strike in the market that day, the Hodja patted the coarse hair of his donkey's neck.

---

1. **myriad:** very many; a great number.

Through the street gate rode the Hodja, and on toward the marketplace. His long legs dangled at the donkey's sides, his feet sometimes touching the cobblestones of the narrow street. It was hard to pass by the charms of market day, but the Hodja had important business on hand. He nodded to right and to left at his many friends in the marketplace, but kept straight on until he reached the animal market.

"Here is a donkey that will make some man proud of his bargain," said the Hodja as he handed the donkey over to the auctioneer.

"Such a good donkey should bring a good price," said the auctioneer. He poked the donkey, pinched its legs, and looked at its teeth. Like the Hodja, he spoke loudly for the benefit of anyone who might be listening.

One after another, the auctioneer led the animals up for sale but not a bid did the Hodja make. His eyes were fixed on one donkey that was bigger, sleeker, and plumper than the others. Surely that was the donkey for him. Finally, all the donkeys were sold but two—the one Nasr-ed-Din Hodja had brought and the one he had **resolved** to ride away. He was relieved to see that the auctioneer led up his old donkey first. It would be good to have the money for his sale jingling in his belt with what money he already had before he started bidding for the beautiful dark donkey on which he had set his heart.

"Here is a donkey worth buying!" The auctioneer rubbed his hands **gloatingly** as he set the Hodja's old donkey before the little group of buyers. "I have watched this donkey many a time and wished it was mine. See that wise look in its eyes! See the gentle way it holds its head! One look at this donkey shows that it would obey your orders before you gave them!"

Nasr-ed-Din Hodja looked at the donkey's eyes. There was a wise look he had never noticed.

"And look at the muscles," the auctioneer droned on. "What loads it could carry! What hills it could climb! Those slim legs mean speed. I **wager** this donkey could run faster than any donkey in Ak Shehir!"

The Hodja looked at the donkey's legs. He had never noticed how strong and slim they were.

"See how smooth this donkey's coat is!" said the auctioneer. "That shows good care. What a pretty shade of gray! What perfectly matching white boots on its feet!"

The Hodja squinted thoughtfully at the donkey. It was prettily marked. Strange he had never noticed.

"How much am I offered for the handsomest, strongest, wisest, gentlest, most industrious donkey in all Ak Shehir?"

"Fifty ghurush," offered a villager.

Nasr-ed-Din Hodja glared at him. Fifty ghurush for the finest donkey in Ak Shehir, indeed!

"Two liras," called the Hodja.

"Two and a half liras," called a villager.

"Three!" The Hodja held up three fingers.

"Four!"

"Five!"

"Six!"

Up and up went the price until a villager bid ten liras.

"Wait a minute!" called the excited Hodja. He grabbed the money bag from his belt and counted his money. Just what he thought! Ten liras and eleven ghurush.

"Ten liras and five ghurush," called a villager.

"Ten liras and eleven ghurush," shouted the Hodja.

He waited. Silence!

"Only ten liras and eleven ghurush for this wonderful donkey!" exclaimed the auctioneer who knew perfectly well that was a good price. "Come, someone! Make it eleven liras."

Everyone waited. Silence!

The auctioneer handed the bridle to Nasr-ed-Din Hodja. The Hodja emptied his money bag into the auctioneer's hand. He threw his long legs over the donkey's back and settled into the familiar saddle.

"Ughr-r-r-r," he whirred to the donkey and off they trotted toward home. How proud of his bargaining Fatima would be!

Halfway home he began wondering why he had an empty money bag. He had planned, by good bargaining, to bring home a donkey and more money than he carried away. It was puzzling. Perhaps Fatima could explain.

And perhaps she did.

SELECTING DETAILS FROM THE STORY.
Each of the following sentences helps
you understand the story. Complete each
sentence below by putting an *x* in the
box next to the correct answer.

1. Nasr-ed-Din Hodja complained that
   his donkey was as
   ☐ a. strong as an ox.
   ☐ b. swift as a deer.
   ☐ c. stubborn as a donkey.

2. The Hodja told his wife that he would
   ☐ a. buy some bread and vegetables
      at the market.
   ☐ b. trade his donkey for a similar
      one.
   ☐ c. sell his donkey, buy a better one,
      and still have plenty of money
      left over.

3. When the auctioneer praised the
   Hodja's donkey, the Hodja
   ☐ a. knew that the auctioneer was only
      trying to bid up the price.
   ☐ b. looked closely at the donkey and
      began to appreciate it.
   ☐ c. complimented the auctioneer for
      doing a fine job.

4. At the end of the story, the Hodja
   ☐ a. gave all of his money to the
      auctioneer.
   ☐ b. realized that he had been
      cheated.
   ☐ c. got into an argument with the
      auctioneer.

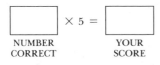

NUMBER CORRECT   YOUR SCORE

HANDLING STORY ELEMENTS. Each of
the following questions reviews your
understanding of story elements. Put
an *x* in the box next to the correct
answer to each question.

1. Nasr-ed-Din Hodja may best be
   characterized as
   ☐ a. very wise.
   ☐ b. quite wealthy.
   ☐ c. foolish.

2. What is the *mood* of "The Donkey Goes
   to Market"?
   ☐ a. sad
   ☐ b. humorous
   ☐ c. frightening

3. The author's *purpose* in writing the
   story was to
   ☐ a. entertain the reader.
   ☐ b. teach the reader.
   ☐ c. convince the reader.

4. Which of the following best tells the
   theme of the story?
   ☐ a. A good donkey can bring a high
      price at the market.
   ☐ b. A man goes to the market to get
      a bargain.
   ☐ c. A clever auctioneer talks a man
      into buying his own donkey.

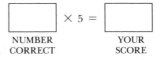

NUMBER CORRECT   YOUR SCORE

OBSERVING NEW VOCABULARY WORDS. Answer the following vocabulary questions by putting an *x* in the box next to the correct answer. The vocabulary words are printed in **boldface** in the story. If you wish, look back at the words before you answer the questions.

1. Fatima patted the donkey, which rubbed its head affectionately against her sleeve. The word *affectionately* means
   ☐ a. stubbornly.
   ☐ b. lovingly.
   ☐ c. drearily.

2. Nasr-ed-Din Hodja was resolved to buy the donkey that was bigger and plumper than the rest. As used here, the word *resolved* means
   ☐ a. determined.
   ☐ b. startled.
   ☐ c. threatened.

3. The auctioneer was willing to wager that the Hodja's donkey could run faster than any other donkey there. What is the meaning of the word *wager*?
   ☐ a. wonder about
   ☐ b. hesitate
   ☐ c. bet

4. "Here is a donkey worth buying!" he said gloatingly, as he rubbed his hands together. The word *gloatingly* means in a
   ☐ a. sorrowful way.
   ☐ b. shocked way.
   ☐ c. boastful way.

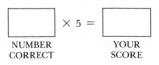

NUMBER CORRECT   × 5 =   YOUR SCORE

COMPLETING A CLOZE PASSAGE. Complete the following paragraph by filling in each blank with one of the words listed in the box below. Each of the words appears in the story. Since there are five words and four blanks, one word in the group will not be used.

The donkey has been _____ the beast of burden. That is because, for hundreds of years, donkeys have been used to pull wagons or carry loads on their _____. While it is true that donkeys can be very _____, this usually occurs when the animal is treated badly. Generally, _____ are quite gentle and make good pets for children.

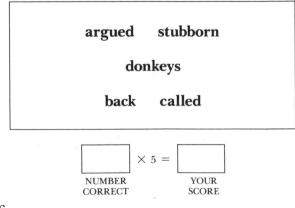

argued   stubborn

donkeys

back   called

NUMBER CORRECT   × 5 =   YOUR SCORE

146

KNOWING HOW TO READ CRITICALLY. Each of the following questions will help you to think critically about the selection. Put an *x* in the box next to the correct answer.

1. Which statement is true?
   - ☐ a. The Hodja's donkey was surely the finest donkey anyone had ever seen.
   - ☐ b. The Hodja was afraid that someone at the market would trick him.
   - ☐ c. The Hodja forgot that he was selling his donkey, not buying it.

2. Fatima said that arguing with her husband was "like throwing dry leaves on a fire." This suggests that
   - ☐ a. arguing with the Hodja only made matters worse.
   - ☐ b. the Hodja usually listened to reason.
   - ☐ c. the Hodja never argued about anything.

3. We may infer that liras and ghurush are
   - ☐ a. kinds of food.
   - ☐ b. units of money.
   - ☐ c. articles of clothing.

4. It is fair to say that
   - ☐ a. Nasr-ed-Din Hodja was very quick thinking.
   - ☐ b. the auctioneer was an excellent salesperson.
   - ☐ c. Fatima was probably pleased with the deal that her husband made.

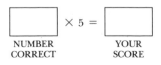

| NUMBER CORRECT | × 5 = | YOUR SCORE |

Questions for Writing and Discussion

- The Hodja told his wife, "You know how good I am about buying and selling." How good was the Hodja at buying and selling? Explain.
- The word *gullible* means "easily deceived or cheated." Explain how the Hodja was gullible.
- At the beginning of the story, the Hodja told his wife, "The next time you see it (the donkey), someone else will be riding it." Show that the author intends that remark to be amusing.

Use the boxes below to total your scores for the exercises. Then write your score on pages 150 and 151.

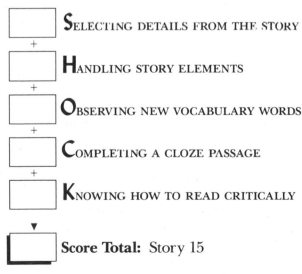

SELECTING DETAILS FROM THE STORY

+

HANDLING STORY ELEMENTS

+

OBSERVING NEW VOCABULARY WORDS

+

COMPLETING A CLOZE PASSAGE

+

KNOWING HOW TO READ CRITICALLY

▼

Score Total: Story 15

Acknowledgments

Acknowledgment is gratefully made to the following publishers, authors, and agents for permission to reprint these works. Adaptations and abridgments are by Burton Goodman.

"Dear Amanda" by Linnah Gary. ©1965 by Scholastic Magazine. Used by permission of Scholastic, Inc.

"The Invaders" by Jack Ritchie. ©1978 by *Boys' Life*. Reprinted by permission of Larry Sternig Literary Agency.

"The Expression" by José Francés. All attempts have been made to locate the copyright holder.

"The Cog" by Charles Fritch. Reprinted by permission of the author and the author's agents, Scott Meredith Literary Agency, Inc., 845 Third Avenue, New York, New York 10022.

"The Scholarship" by Minfong Ho. Text adaptation, as approved by the author, of "The Scholarship" from *Sing to the Dawn* by Minfong Ho.

"Blue Eyes Far Away" by MacKinlay Kantor. Adapted from *Story Teller* by MacKinlay Kantor. ©1967 by MacKinlay Kantor. Used by permission of Doubleday, a division of Bantam Doubleday Dell Publishing Group, Inc.

"The Cow-Tail Switch," folktale from Liberia. From *The Cow-Tail Switch and Other West African Stories* by Harold Courlander and George Herzog. ©1947, 1975 by Harold Courlander. Adaptation reprinted by permission of Henry Holt and Company, Inc.

Progress Chart

1. Write in your score for each exercise.
2. Write in your Score Total.

	S	H	O	C	K	SCORE TOTAL
Story 1						
Story 2						
Story 3						
Story 4						
Story 5						
Story 6						
Story 7						
Story 8						
Story 9						
Story 10						
Story 11						
Story 12						
Story 13						
Story 14						
Story 15						

Progress Graph

1. Write your Score Total in the box under the number for each story.
2. Put an *x* along the line above each box to show your Score Total for that story.
3. Make a graph of your progress by drawing a line to connect the *x*'s.

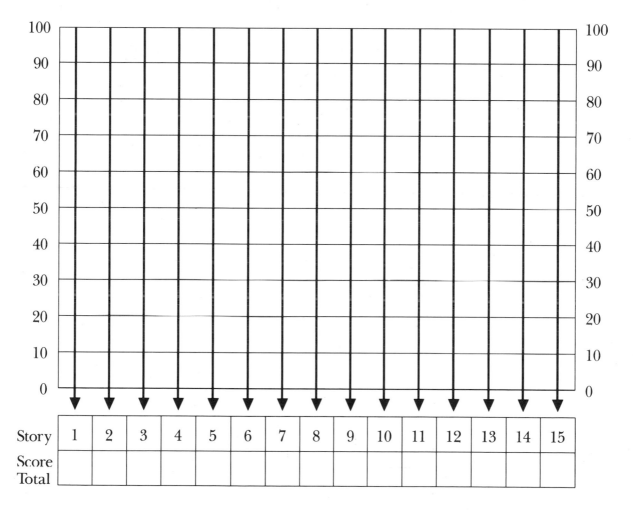

Story	1	2	3	4	5	6	7	8	9	10	11	12	13	14	15
Score Total															